Holy
Desperation

Other Books by Heather King

Parched

Redeemed: Stumbling Toward God, Marginal Sanity, and the Peace That Passes All Understanding

Shirt of Flame: A Year with St. Thérèse of Lisieux

Stumble: Virtue, Vice, and the Space Between

Stripped: At the Intersection of Cancer, Culture, and Christ

Loaded: Money and the Spirituality of Enough

Holy Desperation

PRAYING AS IF YOUR LIFE DEPENDS ON IT

HEATHER KING

LOYOLA PRESS.
A JESUIT MINISTRY
Chicago

LOYOLA PRESS.
A JESUIT MINISTRY

3441 N. Ashland Avenue
Chicago, Illinois 60657
(800) 621-1008
www.loyolapress.com

Cover art credit: Edel Rodriguez (hand and cross), ©iStock.com/Matthew Hertel (grunge texture)

ISBN-13: 978-0-8294-4514-5
ISBN-10: 0-8294-4514-5
Library of Congress Control Number: 2017930455

Printed in the United States of America.
17 18 19 20 21 22 23 Versa 10 9 8 7 6 5 4 3 2 1

To Caryll

Contents

About Fr. Damien

The text from my priest friend, whom I call Fr. Damien, is from several taped conversations I had with him and is used with his permission. I chose to quote him at length, partly in homage to a man who has deeply shaped my own spirituality and partly because his take on the fruits of prayer-based action—and on the confluence of the twelve steps and the Gospels—strikes me as original, moving, and spiritually "true." I've used a pseudonym so as to protect Fr. Damien's privacy and to avoid derogating the twelve-step tradition of anonymity at the level of press, radio, and films.

The thing the church needs most today is the ability to heal wounds and to warm the hearts of the faithful; it needs nearness, proximity. I see the church as a field hospital after battle. It is useless to ask a seriously injured person if he has high cholesterol and about the level of his blood sugars! You have to heal his wounds. Then we can talk about everything else. Heal the wounds, heal the wounds. . . . And you have to start from the ground up.[1]

—Pope Francis

In the Flannery O'Connor novel *Wise Blood*, a backwoods seeker named Enoch Emery steals from the county museum a shrunken mummy who he believes is "the new jesus."

In the Author's Note to the Second Edition, O'Connor noted,

Wise Blood was written by an author congenitally innocent of theory, but one with certain preoccupations. That belief in Christ is to some a matter of life and death has been a stumbling block for readers who would prefer to think it a matter of no great consequence. For them [protagonist] Hazel Motes' integrity lies in his trying with such vigor to get rid of the ragged figure who moves from tree to tree in the back of his mind. For the author, Hazel's integrity lies in his not being able to.[2]

Part One

Crisis

1

The Prayer of Desperation

*All prayer arises from incompetence. Otherwise we would have
no need of it.*

—St. Thérèse of Lisieux

I once did my best to edit a book on prayer that turned out to be one
of the most disturbing, misguided documents I have ever read.

As I worked on this book, I kept thinking, *How do you purport to
know the mind of God, the heart of God?* The really scary thing was that
the guy who'd written it presented himself as a spiritual director.

Finally I said, "Do we really want to be telling people they will go
to hell if they make a 'mistake' in prayer? Do we really want to tell
people God will punish them if they don't pray 'the right' way?"

I said, "You've left no room for the prayer that got me sober. You've
left no room for the prayer of desperation that brought me to God,
then to Christ."

That first prayer of desperation was the Lord's Prayer, said on my
knees in the woods, beneath a pine tree, in back of a friend's house
in Nashville. I was strung out and half-drunk, and I had a cigarette
in my hand. I was thirty-four, and it was the first time in my life I
had ever sincerely prayed. I was sincere because I had just had what
we drunks call a moment of clarity.

The moment of clarity can take many, many different forms and
arise from many situations, but it is basically the moment you admit
to yourself that all your obsessive efforts to manage and control your

life and the people around you so as to engineer an atom of happiness have never worked, are not working now, and are never going to work. It's the moment when you realize that intelligence backed by willpower, the god of our culture, is not only not a god of any sort but also a deeply ineffectual organizing principle. For me, the moment consisted of the realization that if I didn't stop drinking, I was going to die.

So I prayed the prayer, like millions before me, of the atheist in the foxhole. I said the Lord's Prayer, the only prayer besides "Now I lay me down to sleep" that I knew by heart from childhood Sunday school. I put particular emphasis on *Deliver us from evil* because part of my moment of clarity was the knowledge that I faced a power of darkness against which no human power could help me.

I knelt there for a moment. I didn't exactly take the prayer back, but I did start to feel self-conscious. I got up, dusted myself off, went back to the house, and mixed another pitcher of gin-and-tonics. But a few months later, my family had an intervention and shipped me off to a treatment center in Minnesota.

I stayed for thirty days. It took me another year to put down the drugs as well. But from that day to this, I've never had another drink.

You don't have to call God by name. You don't have to believe in him. You don't even have to know you're praying. But if you get on your knees and ask a power greater than you for help, the help will come. It may not come in the form you want or the form you're expecting, but the help will come.

That goes for the drunk with the d.t.'s, the prisoner in solitary confinement, the mother of ten, the missionary nun who feels suicidal, or the priest addicted to porn.

"Ask and you shall receive, seek and you shall find, knock and the door will be opened to you." That is Christ's promise, and Christ never lied.

That is what Christ came for: to be with us in our brokenness and suffering; to help us do a little better. "Blessed are the poor in spirit." "Healthy people don't need a doctor; sick people do." "I came to call not the righteous, but sinners."

So do not let anyone—no spiritual director, no teacher, no family member, no priest even, though we love and revere our priests—ever tell you that you are not allowed to approach Christ exactly as you are, how you are, with every thought, every obsession, every fear, no matter how chaotic, angry, petty, lame, despairing, profane, or crazy.

"Come to me, all you that are weary and are carrying heavy burdens, and I will give you rest" (Matthew 11:28).

Come, all you who have missed the mark, who are dying for lack of meaning, all you who are sick and anxious and lonely and afraid unto death. Come, you who are married to someone you don't love; you who are caring for a parent with Alzheimer's while your siblings play golf; you whose mother is a raging alcoholic; you whose husband, son, or father is a pedophile; you whose daughter is a sex worker. Come, you who live in chronic physical pain, you who are perpetually broke, you who live under a totalitarian dictatorship, you who are pregnant with a baby that's not your husband's or boyfriend's, you who have not been touched by another human being in years, you who live a life of hidden, silent martyrdom that not one other person sees or cares about.

Come close. Come as close as you can.

Heavenly Father, help me believe that I am loved in spite of my ongoing incompetence, littleness, and brokenness. Help me remember that our brokenness is why you came. Help me not be afraid to come close to you, in any way, at any minute of the day or night.

2

Grabbed by the Throat

We can tend to think of prayer as soft, a lullaby. But my own experience has been that I'm usually driven to prayer by a crisis—of meaning, of conscience.

Our Narcotic Culture

We convert because we have an experience that grabs us by the throat and we don't understand why. We puzzle it out in retrospect.[3]
—Dana Gioia, California's poet laureate

We live in a narcotic culture. It is now possible to stay almost completely anesthetized from the first moment of consciousness to our last breath.

I should know. From approximately 1966 to 1986, I moved about the world in a twilight-zone alcoholic haze.

The phenomenon is almost impossible to get across to a normal drinker—one, that is, who can take booze or leave it. But trust me when I say that I'm just as intelligent, driven, disciplined, high minded, hardworking, and kindhearted as you are. Trust me when I say that alcohol has an entirely different effect on me than it does on you.

But I'm an alcoholic. I suffer from the disease of alcoholism.

Thus my first drink, at the age of thirteen, was a religious experience. I felt in complete communion with myself, God, the universe.

That's not the effect alcohol has on a normal drinker.

St. Augustine observed that Satan can't create anything new; he can only destroy or pervert goodness. So the first drink was a faux religious experience. It hooked into my longing for God—which is to say for connection, transcendence, unity, harmony, and love—and corrupted it.

In a way so cunning, baffling, and powerful that only a malevolent intelligence could have conceived it, that first drink also set up an obsession of the mind and a compulsion, a craving, by which I would be held in utter bondage for the next twenty years. That first drink gave me a feeling of connection so compelling that I followed it, as those who suffer from the disease of alcoholics do, almost to the gates of insanity or death.

The Demoniac

Our Lord saves us from the fires of hell, not with a slap, but by touching with a hand that has a nail hole in it.[4]
—Fr. George William Rutler

Christ, with his special heart for the mentally and emotionally ill, constantly cast out demons from the people who came to him. Mark 9:17–29 (NAB) tells one such story:

> Someone from the crowd answered him, "Teacher, I have brought to you my son possessed by a mute spirit. Wherever it seizes him, it throws him down; he foams at the mouth, grinds his teeth, and becomes rigid. I asked your disciples to drive it out, but they were unable to do so."

He said to them in reply, "O faithless generation, how long will I be with you? How long will I endure you? Bring him to me." They brought the boy to him. And when he saw him, the spirit immediately threw the boy into convulsions. As he fell to the ground, he began to roll around and foam at the mouth.

Then he questioned his father, "How long has this been happening to him?" He replied, "Since childhood. It has often thrown him into fire and into water to kill him. But if you can do anything, have compassion on us and help us."

Jesus said to him, "'If you can!' Everything is possible to one who has faith." Then the boy's father cried out, "I do believe, help my unbelief!" Jesus, on seeing a crowd rapidly gathering, rebuked the unclean spirit and said to it, "Mute and deaf spirit, I command you: come out of him and never enter him again!"

Shouting and throwing the boy into convulsions, it came out. He became like a corpse, which caused many to say, "He is dead!" But Jesus took him by the hand, raised him, and he stood up. When he entered the house, his disciples asked him in private, "Why could we not drive it out?"

He said to them, "This kind can only come out through prayer."

This kind can be healed only by prayer. That's the alcoholic.

But the demoniac is also a stand-in for a culture that at every turn numbs without ever really killing our pain, that gluts without satisfying our desperate human hunger.

Our Will Versus God's Will

Still, I'm always afraid that if I turn my will and my life over to God, he'll take away my health insurance. Do something to "build my character." Third-degree burns, maybe, or paralysis.

My friend Dennis *is* paralyzed. He was shot in a random convenience-store holdup forty years ago and has been in a wheelchair ever since. He is among the five most highly evolved human beings I know. He doesn't resent. ("That guy who shot me was doing what he was supposed to do; I was doing what I was supposed to do." "Hate poisons the hater.") He never complains. He never bad-mouths. ("You bad-mouth someone to another, next day that other decides they like the person you bad-mouthed. Bad idea, always.")

He's an incredible storyteller and has a wicked sense of humor. People stop by Dennis's chair to pay their respects, literally. They all but put their hands over their hearts and remove their hats. He's like a head of state.

In other words, being paralyzed is not the worst thing. It's really, really bad. It's intense suffering, but it's not the worst thing.

The worst thing is to live in a state of being so narcotized that we essentially miss our whole life. That narcotized state on the one hand leads us to think that the slightest suffering needs to be medicated. On the other hand, it puts us in a perpetual twilight state that *should* depress us.

Jolted

Before encountering Jesus, Simon could keep his entire life under control. Home, family, fishing—it was easy to keep his little world under control. He was obeyed at home, he was a good fisherman—and in spite of everything, the lake was generous—and the hired hands respected him. But now everything had become unmanageable. Hundreds, thousands of people of every race and language came to ask him for the impossible.[5]
—Dom Mauro-Giuseppe Lepori, O. Cist., abbot general of the
Cistercian Order

For years (during which I somehow managed to earn a law degree and pass the Massachusetts bar), I lived in just such a semicomatose haze of loneliness, depression, self-pity, neurotically self-centered fear, and paralysis.

I suffered from an obsessive-compulsive mental illness against which my intelligence, loving family, discipline, goodwill, longing heart, and drive availed me absolutely nothing. And if that turned out in one way to be the worst thing that ever happened to me, in another way, my alcoholism has turned out to be the best thing that ever happened to me.

I would never, ever have turned to a Power greater than myself unless I absolutely had to. I would never have gotten sober unless my family held an intervention for me and jolted me into the realization that my behavior affected others. In this culture of "rights," entitlement, and perpetual aggrievement, I had come to see myself as a victim, even while I was hurting—if for no other reason, by my utter inability to be present as a human being—everyone around me.

Sometimes we have a part in creating our suffering; sometimes it's imposed on us. The rain falls on the just and the unjust. No one asks to have alcoholism, but at the same time, I came to see later, I was responsible for everything I'd done under its aegis.

Not everyone has alcoholism. But everyone is subject to the cross of the human condition. When your wife runs off with a younger guy, the kid turns to heroin, you're diagnosed with cancer, and you lose your job, all in the same year, the suffering is profound. It seems that this suffering will break you. Basically that's the psychic state of the alcoholic who's hit bottom.

Whatever our state and situation, "the worst thing" is often the crisis that jolts us into another way of being: a death to our egos from which we emerge viewing the universe from a radically new vantage point.

Flannery O'Connor, the great Southern Catholic novelist, wrote stories in which grace often comes through violence. Mrs. May, a smug small-town Pharisee, is gored by a neighbor's bull in "Greenleaf." In "Everything That Rises Must Converge," Julian, a disdainful artiste who lives with his mother and to whom he considers himself vastly superior, insults her one last time, then watches her convulse with a heart attack and die. In "The Lame Shall Enter First," Sheppard, a social worker who has more compassion for a "needy" black boy than his own motherless son discovers that, while watching the heavens through the telescope he's bought to expand the black boy's horizons, his son has hung himself.

In her essay collection *Mystery and Manners*, O'Connor observes:

> When you can assume that your audience holds the same beliefs you do, you can relax a little and use more normal means of talking to it; when you have to assume that it does not, then you have to make your vision apparent by shock—to the hard of hearing you shout, and for the almost-blind you draw large and startling figures.[6]

Bring the Body, and the Mind Will Follow

At birth we set sail into the world with sealed orders.
—Attributed to Søren Kierkegaard

After that intervention, my parents shipped me off for thirty days to a treatment center in Minnesota. *Figures*, I thought, *some kind of prairie evangelical cult camp*, and packed my Jack Daniel's T-shirt.

Sap that I am, within a week I'd fallen in love with the trees and ponds, my fellow female alkies, and the spirit of the place, which had a compelling realness. No one tried to airbrush or whitewash; no one tried to evangelize. We were screwed, we basically agreed. *And* there was hope.

I'd never had anything against God. I just thought God was for people who weren't very smart.

Still, I had to admit that with my law degree, my deep reading of Kafka, Dostoevsky, Baudelaire, and Jean Genet, I was spending my life drinking, recovering from hangovers, and sleeping with illiterate small-time hustlers and crooks. Not just sleeping with, actually—stalking.

At age thirty-four, I had no real idea of how to live. I was terrified of just about all actual human interaction. I was unemployable: I could barely sit up straight for eight hours and thus could work neither as a lawyer nor, any longer, at the kind of shabby waitressing jobs with which I'd supported my drinking "career." I was squandering my inheritance in the mire, like the younger brother in the parable of the prodigal son.

The people at the treatment center didn't evangelize. But they did mention that we might want to make some kind of effort to connect with a Power greater than ourselves—a God, so to speak, of our own understanding.

Of course, this sounded terribly hokey and unsophisticated.

I made the effort anyway—which consisted for the most part in simply being open to the idea of God.

They said, "You don't have to get on your knees, though some of us do." So in my tepid, self-conscious way, I did that, too.

It was only many years later I realized that prayer, among other things, puts us in right relation to reality. The essence of prayer consists in doing what most of us have never done before and that no human being does unless we are utterly, completely out of ideas—and that is to acknowledge defeat and ask for help.

Kneeling, our heads are close to our hearts.

Kneeling, we feel our exhaustion.

Kneeling, we're the height of children.

Identify, Don't Compare

[W]hen you go into a classroom and things are very neat, or into a dormitory and find the room very tidy, with nothing on the floor,

nothing pinned up on the walls, there's something wrong. Because
people are not orderly by nature. They crave for creativity and
liberty. They need to have things on the wall and perhaps their
beds unmade and the place a bit scruffy. This is reality; this is
home; this is people.
People are not terribly neat and orderly; they are not machines
to be polished up so that the shepherd can collect praises for his
tidiness, his capacity. People growing in liberty do not all have the
same haircuts and look the same and wear the same smiles. Each
one is different, each one is growing in his own way, in positive
action, and in love. The flock will sense if the shepherd is
demanding order because he is scared of people, or if he is just
seeking his own power and glory.[7]
—Jean Vanier

I have a priest friend, sober over forty years, whom I'll call Fr.
Damien. He's the king of the one-liner. "Drinking never made me
happy—but it made me feel like I was going to be happy in fifteen
minutes." "The good news is God loves you. The bad news is he
loves everyone else, too." I once asked him how I'd know if I was
making spiritual progress. He thought for a minute. "If crazy people
aren't afraid to come up and talk to you," he replied, "that's a pretty
good sign."

Here's how he describes the beginning of his own spiritual
awakening:

> When I was getting sober, there was a moment I'll of course
> describe inadequately. I was in Sterling, New Jersey. After six treat-
> ments and detoxes, I got to go back on the airplane and get with
> these guys, fellow priests. And it was, fortunately for me, a very
> badly run house. It had this one unrecovered Al-Anon big bossy
> guy who would go give retreats on the weekends to Al-Anons and
> leave two hapless brothers opening cans of peas and carrots and

beets for the meals. And we would go to meetings. We were supposed to go to three a week, but I went every day because meetings were the only place you could go! And you paid two dollars out of your pocket. To go to a meeting! You had to pay up, gas money. This was not one of those gleaming vans. Pay up and take the Green Hornet, we called it. It wasn't even a Hornet, it was a Plymouth. We went on the Erie Lackawanna train every Tuesday through Newark to Hoboken, under the river, to go to a meeting with all the priests in Brooklyn and Manhattan. We had to go to a meeting. Wonderful Tuesday off. Had to wear your Roman collar and a black suit, it was winter. So you had this black suit, and a cap, and a plaid scarf so you could cover your collar and go to a movie on 42nd Street. See museums, visit places.

Anyway, I went to a meeting every day. We also had a few things in the house, lectures from a therapist and some guy who knew drug and alcohol chemistry. White hair, blue blazer, I liked his lectures, or I liked them enough. They were fine. So I'm just starting to sleepwalk into, Okay I'll do it, I have the time, and I'm hanging out with the guys more or less all day. I was there five months. And three or four months into it, and this reflection came thirty years later: I cheered up.

I cheered up. The picture that comes to mind is of a guy sharing other than myself. I was identifying with people. But this time I loved him. I had a joy. [Tears up]. He's alive and so am I. That's the deal. I'm being dragged into this. It isn't a perfect life and it's going to be filled with all kinds of ambiguities and secrets and bad habits, but this is . . . there's something at the core of what happens when you pay attention to the steps and go to meetings that draws you. The bud blooms and you become a human being who is actually alive while you do regular things. While you're doing regular things you begin to identify at a much higher percentage . . . when you identify, you also compare, and comparing wrecks it. But if the energy of identifying just goes past 50 percent, love is winning. Life is winning.

We have that in us in our better moments, to identify a little more than to compare. When that happens, you go sane. And you know it's all right. You have a life. That's the way I picture it. It's hope. You can have your bad days, and there are some people who drive you nuts but you're living a life. When you drink the whole thing is cut down. You cannot identify in a way that touches your heart and gives you life. Alcohol cuts down the system you need to identify with people. So when you're not drinking and it's negativity mostly, and the self-centered aspect edges other things out, you don't have the joy or the skip in the step; the move that's spontaneous, that doesn't require any willed action.

When you're identifying more than comparing, you're in a dance, you and life. And as you get into that move, that dance, something in the middle of your person says, This is very healthy. You can have a life now. If you're 50.2 percent into identifying, you get to live. You get to live.

I find delightful this idea that a spiritual awakening consists in our ability to rejoice at the awakening of *another*. My narcissistic psyche can delude me into thinking that a spiritual awakening is about *my* edification, my progress, my psychic comfort, security, and peace. Whereas genuine spiritual awakening seems to consist in a disappearance, however temporary, of self.

There's nothing in authentic spiritual awakening of "I'm doing it better than the next person." The sense is, "I'll be darned. I actually got out of my own way long enough to see that I am capable of loving another, of admiring and celebrating someone else!"

The sign of the follower of Christ is not necessarily that we have only "healthy relationships" and our checkbooks are balanced and our children are going to Ivy League schools. The sign of the follower of Christ is that we get a kick out of life.

We Cheer Up. We Get to Live.

We draw people to Christ not by loudly discrediting what they believe, by telling them how wrong they are and how right we are,

*but by showing them a light that is so lovely that they want with
all their hearts to know the source of it.*[8]

—Madeleine L'Engle

That month at Hazelden in 1986 saved my life. To this day I can't
pinpoint when or where—but sometime during those thirty days, the
obsession to drink was lifted.

I never had a "white light" experience. The best I can figure was
that, deep below the level of consciousness, I *consented* for the obsession to be removed. I consented to believe I could let alcohol go and
still live. I consented for my identity as a drinker, my organizing principle, to die.

However and whenever it happened, the lifting of that obsession
remains forever the central fact of my existence. That's why, when I
came into the Church nine years later, the paradigm of Crucifixion
and Resurrection, the parable of the prodigal son, the conscience-
based teachings, the merciful God who also assumes you're going to
be willing to step up to the plate and contribute—all that made perfect sense to me.

The recovery to which I was invited suggested an ongoing search
for a Power greater than myself, a searching moral inventory, the sharing of the inventory with another, a concerted effort to make the people I'd harmed whole, an ongoing, minute-by-minute examination of
conscience, the development of a disciplined practice of prayer and
meditation, and a life of service.

To say that nothing in any of that struck me as remotely promising
would be an understatement. But because I was out of ideas, and
against my better judgment, and with much grumbling but also a
strange secret joy, in my klutzy way I followed along.

In my klutzy way, I've been following along ever since.

The life I've been given has turned out to be nothing I would or could have imagined—and exactly the life I wanted.

Lord, help me be willing to be grabbed by the throat and jolted out of my complacency. Deliver me from the low-level anesthetic haze of distractions and false gods in which I live. Help me identify with the hunger and poverty of my fellows rather than compare their wealth and accomplishments to mine.

3

What Do We Mean by God?

I, for one, tend to assume without close questioning that everyone sees God essentially as I do. Of course, I'm very wrong.

I Don't Believe in the God You Don't Believe in Either

Go to a clear window—as you would with a book with small print—and seek meetings with holy men and women so that you may see clearly your own heart.[9]
—Palladius of Galatia

Let me back up for a minute, because I think many of us get stuck, and much misunderstanding occurs, over a question that seldom ever gets asked out loud: What do we mean by *God*?

Fr. Damien, my priest friend in recovery, is often approached by people with anti-God baggage.

> I commonly tell them, "You know that God that you don't want anything to do with? I don't want anything to do with that God either. The reference to the God you just used—I don't believe in that God either. I don't believe in the God you don't believe in. We're together on that. I'm right with you on that."
>
> Then I tell them to turn it into an indirect thing. Try to get back a little bit. Don't look for *God*. Look first for faith in some people

who you identify with and who have a little sense and who you like. And then go from there, and they'll let you know that they don't *get* God either and that they're in on something that has to do with a Power greater than themselves and that gives them some light and encouragement.

In other words, don't look for God, look for other people's experience of God. There are some people who say, "I have a God" and you think, rightly, "Well, I don't want to have anything to do with that God." If they're crazy or cruel, for example, not a good sign. Don't join that group.

There are other people who probably don't even talk about God a whole lot, but they're a deep encouragement to you by their spirit, their attitude, their behavior, their way of life. If you asked them, "Do you believe in God?" they'd say, "Oh yeah. I don't have much to say about Him but oh yeah. Definitely. I at least know about his friends. The saints, the Bible."

But faith isn't just about knowing about God. Who cares if you've memorized a bunch of Gospel passages but are still trying to lord it over? Faith is a relationship that encourages you to come alive or to have some kind of sense in your life. Aliveness is the big deal. To help you deal with the problem of evil, the problem of limitations we have. We don't get to capture God, take him home, and make some money off Him. We have to be worshipers. We have the same need to have faith, and to be encouraged and admonished by God.

Our mentors, our heroes, our sponsors, our saints are people who have had as far as we can tell an authentic spiritual experience. As they tell their stories, as they talk to us, they won't go beyond the parameters of what they really know. But they also won't say, "Oh, it's unknowable so just forget about the whole thing." In so many words, they'll say, "I don't *own* God, but I've had an experience that I'm dying to share with you."

The German theologian Karl Rahner's "Blessed Despair" is the most important single page I know of the practical implications of the transcendence, and the immanence, of God. Transcendence: beyond the horizon of being. Beyond the horizon of what is speakable and conceivable. Got it? *Beyond the universe.* But don't whine about this, Rahner says. Get over it! Adjust! The immanence of God means he's closer to you than you are to yourself—and you can't get in there, either! Yup. That's the deal! Settle for the expression of people's spiritual experience. You're not going to get around God or inside God, and don't cry about it. Be respectful of the mystery of God. Both closer to you than you are to yourself and beyond the horizon of being. In our human condition, both these dimensions—the immanent and the transcendent—are inescapable . . . we're absolutely in *need* of God. But let God be God.

In other words, we seek and quest with all our hearts. But we never get to grasp God, own God, have a corner on God. That can't be the goal of our seeking. We have our eyes and ears open for the person who seems, in some very understated, quiet way, to have caught fire with God.

At least that is how it has worked out for me. All the people I quote here, all the books, art, music I've been led to, have been the fruit of my seeking. All—Fr. Damien being a prime example—are characterized by this quiet fire that attracts rather than promotes, markets, or sells.

Don't Look for God, Look for People Who Seem to Have Had an Experience of God

Charles Dickens understood the difference between mercy and what he called "telescopic philanthropy." Mercy brings together flesh and blood. Telescopic philanthropy keeps them conveniently far apart. Mercy costs us in sweat and time. Mercy demands that we listen even to the rambles of a bad or sick man. Telescopic philanthropy pretends to pay a human debt by a sort of business exchange, a clean deal.[10]

—Anthony Esolen

I used to get all exercised, thinking that I was posing a deep and original existential question by asking, How about the mother in sub-Saharan Africa whose child is *dying of AIDS?* How about the man in the *Nazi concentration camp?*

Suffering *is* a deep existential question, but I overlooked the fact that those with some kind of faith are often using it to pray and as best they can to help others. I was more outraged on behalf of others who were suffering than they often seemed to be themselves.

For instance, take Leymah Gbowee (b. 1972), the Nobel Peace Prize–winning activist who, under a brutal dictatorship and amidst bands of murderously marauding warlords, spearheaded a movement known as Women of Liberia Mass Action for Peace that helped over-throw Charles Taylor (later convicted of crimes against humanity) and galvanized the women of Liberia to help stop the violence that was destroying their children. "If any changes were to be made in soci-ety," she realized, "it had to be by the mothers." She was encouraged and mentored by Lutheran pastors, Martin Luther King Jr., Gandhi, and the teachings of Christ.

Take Fr. Alfred Delp (1907–1945), a German convert and priest who fell into the hands of the Nazis during World War II. His crime, as he observed, consisted simply in being a Jesuit.

He awaited trial in solitary confinement, with his hands shackled. During his incarceration, he managed to work one hand free and to write, among other things, a series of Advent meditations.

Sentenced to death, awaiting execution, Fr. Delp didn't indulge in self-pity, recriminations, or thoughts of vengeance. He apologized to those to whom he'd been unkind. Then he wrote, "I will honestly and patiently await God's will. I will trust him till they come to fetch me. I will do my best to ensure that this blessing, too, shall not find me broken and in despair."[11]

Fr. Delp was executed by hanging on February 2, 1945. The Nazis scattered his ashes over a manure field. His beatification process was begun in 1990.

Take Emma Hauck, a married mother of two who, confined to a German mental institution with schizophrenia, wrote thousands of times the anguished plea, *Sweetheart, come.* The plea turned out to have been directed to her husband, Mark, and the sheets of paper on which she wrote it are now enshrined as "outsider art."

These people weren't outraged *against God.* They seemed to live out of a kind of trust that to the outsider appears borderline crazy. They seem to be looking beyond their immediate situation to another realm.

God the Suitor

God is like a person who clears his throat while hiding and so gives himself away.[12]

—Meister Eckhart

I've met people who loved gardening or fishing or the saxophone: beautiful, hardworking, talented people with noble hearts. They think they can't find God. They'll ask, "Where is God? When is God going to come?"

We've been given this insane gift of life. We're living in the midst of the Resurrection. And all day, all night, still our hearts ask, *Where is God?*

Early in my sobriety I began to realize that God was the things, or in or behind the things, or had created the things, that I'd loved my whole life. Bach cantatas, all flowers, all birds. The man or woman who suffered and who didn't complain and who tried to help the next person.

Oh—*that's* God. The blue heron. The trees that changed color in fall. That swelling in my heart when the tattooed guy with three months of sobriety choked up as he said, "My wife cut me out of her life, but she's gonna let me see my two-year-old daughter. *I'm gonna see my little girl next week.*"

I've also met people who were never going to cross the threshold of any church and who had a deep God-consciousness. "God is polite!" they'd say wonderingly. Or longingly, "I want a God with a face!" or "You know what I realized yesterday? God isn't mad at me! I always thought God was mad at me."

We're all onto something. As Meister Eckhart observed, God is like a suitor. He never forces himself on us, but if we have eyes to see, he's everywhere. "Hey, over here, check it out: a ruby-throated humming-bird!" "Hello there, you with the heavy heart, look, a sunrise!" "Yoo-hoo, I know you think no one loves you, but look, this beggar man is dying to touch your hand!"

Things changed for me when I began to see that *I had always loved God* and that what I did each morning—that sitting quietly watching the light, listening to the sparrows, feeling incoherently grateful, let-ting my mind wander to the mysteries of the universe—was prayer.

On February 23, 1944, Anne Frank wrote in her diary,

> Nearly every morning I go to the attic . . . to blow the stuffy air out of my lungs. From my favorite spot on the floor I look up at the blue sky and the bare chestnut tree, on whose branches lit-tle raindrops shine, appearing like silver, and at the seagulls and other birds as they glide on the wind. . . . "As long as this exists," I thought, "and I may live to see it, this sunshine, the cloudless skies, while this lasts I cannot be unhappy."[13]

That's a form of prayer. That's evidence of a contemplative, questing heart. That's a capacity and love for beauty that is one of the surest signs that prayer has already taken deep root. That capacity to love the chestnut tree was why, crammed with seven other family members and friends into her Secret Annex, hunted by the Nazis, that young girl who would die in the camps could write, "I still believe, in spite of everything, that people are good at heart." Anne Frank had tapped into the living God.

Again, you don't have to call him by name. That's how humble God is. He'd way rather we get sober and help another alcoholic, or feel the joy and wonder of a chestnut tree, than that we call him by name.

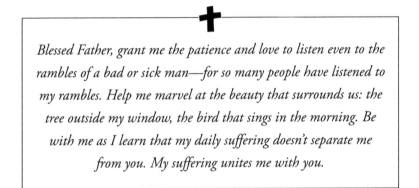

Blessed Father, grant me the patience and love to listen even to the rambles of a bad or sick man—for so many people have listened to my rambles. Help me marvel at the beauty that surrounds us: the tree outside my window, the bird that sings in the morning. Be with me as I learn that my daily suffering doesn't separate me from you. My suffering unites me with you.

4

The Set-Aside Prayer

Being open-minded doesn't mean ceding our intelligence, discernment, or powers of discrimination. Open-mindedness, rather, connotes the childlike heart that is able to welcome a new experience. Honesty and willingness go toward the capacity to imagine a whole new way of seeing and being in the world.

Open-Mindedness, Honesty, Willingness

For I was hungry and you gave me food, I was thirsty and you gave
me something to drink, I was a stranger and you welcomed me, I
was naked and you gave me clothing, I was sick and you took care
of me, I was in prison and you visited me.
—Matthew 25:35–36

I used to think I was open-minded because I'd invite the cabdriver upstairs. No, no, that's not open-mindedness. That's promiscuity. That's *looseness*.

The open-mindedness, honesty, and willingness required in our quest for God seem to involve an imagination that's willing to catch fire: a capacity to be moved, to be touched, to have a sense of humor about ourselves; a taste for the wild-card surprise; and a profound awareness of our vulnerability, brokenness, and need.

Early in my sobriety, someone suggested a beautifully human prayer for anyone who is searching for God: the Set-Aside Prayer. You can adapt it any way you like. This is more or less the one I came up with:

Dear God, Please set aside everything I know or think I know about spirituality, religion, and especially about you, God. Set aside every idea that has frightened, enraged, threatened, or repulsed me. Set aside everything that's been forced down my throat, that's inconsistent, that has traumatized me. Set aside all my righteous indignation at religious hypocrisy, at the fact that children suffer, at my own hemorrhaging wounds, at my doubt, fear, guilt, bewilderment, shame, loneliness, confusion, despair, lust, jealousy, and rage. Set aside these things so that I may have an open mind and a new experience.

Be careful what you ask for, as they say. What happened for me was that, working as a Beverly Hills attorney—a job I feared and loathed unto death—I somehow ended up taking my childhood Bible with me to work. And I read the Gospels.

Feed My Sheep

When they had finished breakfast, Jesus said to Simon Peter, "Simon son of John, do you love me more than these?" He said to him, "Yes, Lord; you know that I love you." Jesus said to him, "Feed my lambs."
A second time he said to him, "Simon son of John, do you love me?" He said to him, "Yes, Lord; you know that I love you." Jesus said to him, "Tend my sheep."
He said to him the third time, "Simon son of John, do you love me?" Peter felt hurt because he said to him the third time, "Do you love me?" And he said to him, "Lord, you know everything; you know that I love you." Jesus said to him, "Feed my sheep."
—John 21:15–17

I already had the experience of getting sober in a fellowship of drunks. That experience dovetailed at every juncture with the Christ of the Gospels I was meeting, with increasing excitement, on the sixth floor of a Beverly Hills office building at the corner of Wilshire Boulevard and Doheny Drive in the early nineties.

"How can you say to your neighbor, 'Let me take the speck out of your eye,' while the log is in your own eye? You hypocrite, first take the log out of your own eye, and then you will see clearly to take the speck out of your neighbor's eye" (Matthew 7:4–5). "Let your word be 'Yes, Yes' or 'No, No'; anything more than this comes from the evil one" (Matthew 5:37). "Do not think that I have come to abolish the law or the prophets; I have come not to abolish but to fulfill" (Matthew 5:17).

And he fulfilled it in the most unlikely, radical, counterintuitive way! He turned everything on its head *and* brought it a level higher in a way that was both infinitely challenging and infinitely surprising.

"Thou shalt not kill" became "Love thine enemies."

"Thou shalt not steal" became "If a man asks for your cloak, give him your tunic as well."

"Thou shalt have no other gods before me" became "Do you love me? Then feed my sheep. Tend my lambs."

As Fr. Damien describes the similarly counterintuitive phenomenon of getting sober:

> We welcome you, and we also recognize you as a child of God with the dignity of any other person on earth. We're judging you to be a person of high standards, a person who will not be satisfied with acting from a heart that's anything less than entirely free. And we have some principles of loving, honest, responsible behavior that we suggest you follow. You'll stay welcome even if you don't follow them, but—here's the thing: you won't care. You won't care that you're welcome; you'll miss out on all the wonder, the love, the growth.

I began to realize he could just as well be talking about becoming a member of the Church.

I'd recently watched a friend die of cirrhosis. If you've ever sat with someone who is dying, you know that the diminishment, the floating off to something that on this side we can't know or imagine, is a holy, holy thing. All the jockeying for status, the resentments, the wondering how we're presenting ourselves melt away. We get to draw close to that person, as close as we often longed to be in life but because of our respective fears, blocks, and wounds, couldn't.

When you're that poor, everyone gets to approach. Flannery O'Connor entitled one of her short stories, "You Can't Be Any Poorer Than Dead." I saw that this was how poor Christ became for our sakes. We had a God who pitched his tent among us, let us kill him, and *still* said, "Come to me, all you that are weary and are carrying heavy burdens, and I will give you rest" (Matthew 11:28). Who *still* told us that we're loved so much that every hair on our heads is numbered (Matthew 10:30). Who still said, "Truly I tell you, today you will be with me in Paradise" (Luke 23:43).

I'd lived my whole life thinking that love had to be earned by being smart, by being good, and also, perversely, by selling myself short at every turn.

Fr. Damien describes this by saying,

Some of us have a deeply misguided desire to be saved through excellence. We want to be spontaneous yet profound, highly intelligent yet down-to-earth, well-balanced yet passionate, dignified but self-deprecating. We want to be physically fit, good-looking, calm in the face of tragedy, suave in the face of heartbreak, and to have really, really good skin. Through the Incarnational mystery of being broken open by our fellow alcoholics and addicts, we forget about all that. We become what we really wanted to be all along: we become human. We realize the real point of sobriety is to get in good enough shape to help another alcoholic.

I began to see that the purpose of a relationship with God, of prayer, wasn't to "be good." It was to help out.

Or as Pope Francis observes, "I see the church as a field hospital after battle. . . . Heal the wounds, heal the wounds."

Gratitude Made Holy

*One of my greatest experiences! Lord God, that beauty! They
circled over me for a long time. Disappeared into the solar haze
like a gleaming, silver ribbon. . . . That this should have happened
to me, who have so long been the outsider.*[14]
—from the diary of composer Jean Sibelius, after seeing sixteen
swans flying in formation over Ainola, his Finnish home

In 1990, I'd moved from the Boston area to L.A. with my new (now ex-) husband, a lovely man who was on his own spiritual quest but not terribly interested in mine.

In RCIA (the Rite of Christian Initiation of Adults), the program by which the Catholic church prepares adult converts, I learned that a sacrament is that which signifies that which it brings into being. The Eucharist signifies love, and it brings into being more love. Confession signifies mercy and forgiveness, and it brings into being more mercy and forgiveness.

A friend in AA who also converted describes the Eucharist like this:

We give chips to mark periods of sobriety: 30, 60, and 90 days; six months, nine months. To the outsider that's just a cheap plastic poker chip. But if you're sober, you know that chip carries all the sobriety, all the fellowship, all the love of every drunk who's come before you, every drunk now, and every drunk who'll come after. You know you're taking the chip not so much for yourself, or not just for yourself, but for everyone who's trying to get sober, everyone who died drunk, and really for everyone, period. Because it's a good, good thing for a drunk to get and stay sober. It helps out everybody, everywhere.

That's something of what the Eucharist is to me. But it's not just a symbol. It's Real. Not literal, not virtual, not actual, but the Real Body of Christ. His love made it Real; our love, our desire for love, our participation, continues to make it Real. Our desire for it to be so helps make it so. We're saved, we're nourished, we pass it on.

For my own part, I had no problem whatsoever with the Virgin Birth, the Resurrection of Christ, or the belief that by the consecration during the Mass, the Host becomes the Real Body of Christ: love incarnate, love made holy, love not captured but safeguarded and cherished and multiplied; love held and broken and consumed and passed on, for two thousand unbroken years.

No one knows better than a drunk who's been struck sober that things happen on a level we can't see.

In 1994, I quit that job as a lawyer to follow my vocation of writing. In 1996, I came into the Church. In 2001, my husband and I were divorced. The marriage was later annulled.

Twenty years after having come into the Church, working with other drunks is a big part of my daily practice. It's the place where I most often see the Gospels lived out in others, and experience living them out myself.

Every morning I also watch the sun rise, listen to the birds, and spend an hour or so in prayer. I pray the Divine Office. I read that day's liturgy. I trudge to Mass and confession, like so many of us, alone.

I'm sixty-four, single, childless.

At the altar, I kneel in gratitude for my sobriety, my life. At the altar, my gratitude is consecrated.

The words *accompany* and *companion* come from the Latin *cum panis*: "with bread." Bread, the broken and shared Body of Christ, is at the heart of the Eucharist.

At the altar, I worship before the God who walks with us.

The Reality behind This One

There can be no doubt that as a matter of fact a religious life, exclusively pursued, does tend to make the person exceptional and eccentric. I speak now not of your ordinary religious believer, who follows the conventional observances of his country. . . . It would profit us little to study this second-hand religious life.[15]

—William James

One thing I love about Catholicism is that it attracts nutcases. Otherwise, how could there be a place for me?

I love it all: Mass, the angels and saints, holy days, incense, candles, bloody statues, relics, pilgrimages. I especially love that miracles—and the "simple," "deluded" people who claim to have experienced them—tend to drive nonbelievers mad.

In *The Cure Within: A History of Mind-Body Medicine*, Anne Harrington describes how "two former rivals from the world of French hysteria and hypnosis research, [Hippolyte] Bernheim and Jean-Martin Charcot, found themselves united in mutual indignation" against the miracles at Lourdes, where a peasant girl had seen a series of apparitions of the Virgin Mary and to this day pilgrims flock for the supposedly healing waters:

All the healings at Lourdes, extraordinary though they were, were simply evidence that the natural healing powers of the mind were far more extensive than the medical profession had previously appreciated. Why had it taken Lourdes to reveal this? [Neurologist/ psychologist] Charcot focused on the remarkable features of

Lourdes as a site. Its remoteness meant that all pilgrims underwent a long, arduous journey to reach it (the train trip from Paris at that time took twenty-two hours). When they finally arrived, they were exhausted and their critical faculties were diminished. Arriving at the grotto itself, they were then immediately immersed in multiple sacred symbols of healing. Joining crowds of other believers, they were infected with the emotional contagion of collective hope. It all added up to a fabulous confluence of factors guaranteed to open the mind to any and all influences. Indeed, others besides Charcot had marveled over this feature of Lourdes: "What medical hypnotist can produce a stage set like this?" exclaimed the physician Félix Regnault.[16]

What medical hypnotist indeed? I once read a *Vanity Fair* interview with Johnny Depp in which he said, "I was always fascinated by people who are considered completely normal, because I find them the weirdest of all."[17]

Absolutely! I thought. *Try hanging out at daily Mass.* Nothing looks tamer from the outside, and nothing is weirder, more violent, more glorious, mysterious, and sublime, than Mass—and the people who participate in it.

Depth psychologist Robert Johnson observed,

> The Catholic Mass is a masterpiece of balancing our cultural life. If one has the courage to see, the Mass is full of the darkest things: there is incest, betrayal, rejection, torture, death—and worse. All this leads to revelation but not until the dark side has been portrayed as vividly as possible. If one went to Mass in high consciousness one would tremble at the awfulness of it—and be redeemed by its balancing effect. . . . One ought to be pale with terror at the Mass.[18]

At the same time, as Flannery O'Connor noted, "Mass could be said out of a suitcase in a furnace room, and the same sacrifice would take place."[19]

There's so much not to like: bad music, bad art, bad homilies. But so what? That I should be allowed to be present at the Holy of holies, the reenactment of the greatest miracle that has ever or will ever or could ever take place: that God took on human flesh and pitched his tent among us!

The Church keeps us nutcases from spinning off into isolated weirdness. You can't get so weird that you're unable to communicate on a simple, human-to-human level. You can't think you're so "original" that no one understands you.

Everyone understands a basically compassionate heart.

Everyone understands the person who will sit down and listen.

Everyone, deep in his or her heart, feels the fundamental urge to worship.

Mysterious Objects

The Christian of the future will be a mystic or will not exist at all.[20]

—Fr. Karl Rahner

My understanding of a mystic isn't someone who sits around day-dreaming all day, though I'm a huge champion of daydreaming. I also pay my bills, change my oil, and meet my deadlines. Mysticism is not antithetical to reality. Mysticism *underlies* reality.

A mystic is someone who sees, and who is constantly on the look-out for, the reality behind this one. And the reality behind this one is love.

Van Gogh, for example, wrote,

Just as we take a train to go to Tarascon or Rouen, we take death to go to a star. What's certainly true in this argument is that, while *alive, we cannot* go to a star, any more than once dead we'd be able to take the train. So it seems to me not impossible that cholera, the stone, consumption, cancer are celestial means of locomotion, just as steamboats, omnibuses and the railway are terrestrial ones.

To die peacefully of old age would be to go there on foot.[21]

The painter Paul Cézanne observed, of a "noble silver olive tree" that grew outside his studio, "It's a living human, it knows all of my life and gives me wonderful advice. I would like to be buried at its feet."[22]

In *Creativity: The Perfect Crime*, Philippe Petit—the high-wire artist who, before 9/11, walked a tightrope between the World Trade Center towers—put it like this:

> I believe in outside forces and influences, I believe in the personality of the elements. I believe in the aliveness of things seemingly inanimate.
>
> You already know of my belief that certain objects have a soul: my top hat, my three juggling balls and my steel wire-rope. I also recognize the aliveness of certain other man-made structures (a cathedral, a skyscraper) as well as nature's creations (trees, mountains, waterfalls).
>
> I am convinced that what surrounds us sometimes emits secret messages that beg to be deciphered, for our own good to guide us, to help us, to protect us. This is why I wrote a chapter titled "Meeting the Gods" in the book on my WTC walk. In it, I recall how I summoned the air, the void, the towers, the wire, the balancing-pole, even my slippers, to lend their assertive presence to my journey. To add their godlike powers to the walk.
>
> In my opinion, not all objects have life. But I am convinced that the ones that do, receive that life from us. The baton of a (possessed) orchestra conductor, the chisel of a (transcendental) sculptor, the balancing-pole of an (illuminated) wire-walker . . .
>
> Part of my faith is to acknowledge that the faith lent to me by these elements or objects is going to serve my pursuit rather than turn against it!
>
> To protect that faith, I never insult these "sacred beings" by openly denying their aliveness. When a moment of doubt concerning their existence arises, I keep it secret. . . .

I believe in the unbelievable. . . .

(Parentheses here to salute "impossible things": things, objects and, why not, animals or people that carry within them a mystery that seems impossible to decode. I make sure my life is kept on a razor's edge of excitement and intrigue by surrounding myself with such mysterious objects).[23]

Cézanne, van Gogh, and Petit give us mystical insights, hearts, lives.

I, too, surround myself with "mysterious objects": prayer cards, Lux Perpetua candles, puppets, dolls, wood carvings, misshapen pottery bowls, flaking gold icons.

These are not just aesthetic, interior-design choices. The objects reflect my understanding that to be a mystic is to believe, and to order our lives on the fact that things happen on a level we can't see.

When my late friend Fred was unconscious in the hospital, for example, I visited anyway, even though he didn't "know" I was there: I believed that mattered; I believed that helped.

I lay a place at my dining room table for the uninvited guest. I dress and comb my hair before showing up at my desk each morning, even if I'm not planning to leave the apartment till afternoon. I don't go to Mass just for myself. I go for the people who hunger for the Eucharist and can't get to it: people in solitary confinement, people too sick to swallow. I go because to celebrate Mass means to walk with the suffering Christ, and that means to walk with all people who are suffering. I go because I believe that small, unseen acts can affect a universal psycho-spiritual shift. The martyrs died for that belief. Christ went to the cross for that belief.

On my desk are two three-by-five cards. One is the sublime Rembrandt *Head of Christ* (1648) that hangs in the Philadelphia Museum of Art. The other is a photo of St. Thérèse of Lisieux where she's looking straight into the camera with a look that combines fixed, intense suffering with the merest shadow of a smile.

Those faces convict me—in a good way.

They say, Really? You're going to be *that* petty?

Eternal Father, let me keep my gaze on you and the things that endure, not on the passing things of this world. At the same time, let me love the beauty of thy house. Let me discover that, if my heart is sufficiently childlike, every good material object can reflect your glory. And, Father, please don't ever, ever, let me lose my sense of humor.

Part Two

Death: To Our Old Ideas and Supposed Unlovability

5

"Stay Awake!"

God's call to us isn't so much primarily to be "good" as to come awake—for in coming awake, we will naturally want to be good, whole, and true. We will naturally want to throw all caution aside and embark on a lifelong pilgrimage. How do we know we're not making it all up? The universe presses back.

The Parable of the Wise and Foolish Virgins

Then the kingdom of heaven will be like this. Ten bridesmaids took their lamps and went to meet the bridegroom. Five of them were foolish, and five were wise. When the foolish took their lamps, they took no oil with them; but the wise took flasks of oil with their lamps. As the bridegroom was delayed, all of them became drowsy and slept. But at midnight there was a shout, "Look! Here is the bridegroom! Come out to meet him." Then all those bridesmaids got up and trimmed their lamps. The foolish said to the wise, "Give us some of your oil, for our lamps are going out." But the wise replied, "No! there will not be enough for you and for us; you had better go to the dealers and buy some for yourselves." And while they went to buy it, the bridegroom came, and those who were ready went with him into the wedding banquet; and the door was shut. Later the other bridesmaids came also, saying, "Lord, lord, open to us." But he replied, "Truly I

tell you, I do not know you." Keep awake therefore, for you know
neither the day nor the hour.
—Matthew 25:1–13

Nothing is more annoying than these so-called sages who sit in a cave going, *La-la-la-la-la, there is no suffering. It's all in your head. Everything is an illusion.*

I always want to get a hammer and start nailing one of their hands to a board. Suffering may be the realest thing in the universe.

Just before he died, Christ said, "Peace I leave with you; my peace I give to you. I do not give to you as the world gives. Do not let your hearts be troubled, and do not let them be afraid" (John 14:27).

Peace as the world gives is a narcotic peace. The peace of Christ often comes in the midst of intense suffering, intense peril.

Personally, I don't particularly want to be balanced or calm. I don't want the kind of peace the world gives. I want to be fully alive and fully awake.

I want to keep my lamp in enough oil so that I can see.

Staring with a Frantic Intentness Outwards

No two ideals could be more opposite than a Christian saint in a
Gothic cathedral and a Buddhist saint in a Chinese temple. The
opposition exists at every point; but perhaps the shortest statement of it
is that the Buddhist saint always has his eyes shut, while the Christian
saint always has them very wide open. The Buddhist saint has a sleek
and harmonious body, but his eyes are heavy and sealed with sleep.
The medieval saint's body is wasted to its crazy bones, but his eyes are
frightfully alive. . . . The Buddhist is looking with a peculiar
intentness inwards. The Christian is staring with a frantic
intentness outwards.[24]
—G. K. Chesterton

The goal of prayer, in other words, is not calm. It is not equanimity. The life of prayer is not about "balance." Was van Gogh "balanced"? Was Beethoven "sane"? Did Mother Teresa ever use the phrase "self-care"?

Self-care in our culture means eating organic food while delivering our bodies, brains, and souls into the care of pharmaceutical companies who produce morning-after pills, children in a dish, and morphine with which we now encourage end-of-life doctors to kill us. Balance in our culture means yoga in the morning, a visit to the therapist in the afternoon, and a Klonopin at night.

The follower of Christ has a healthy disregard for his or her body. As Chesterton also observed, "There is more simplicity in the man who eats caviar on impulse than in the man who eats grape-nuts on principle."[25]

There's no formula. You might fast one day; you might feast the next. You might rest up from time to time; you might burn yourself out. You probably won't much notice.

I'm with Barbara Holland (1933–2010), who wrote about the joys of drinking, smoking, bacon, and naps:

"I was getting sick and tired of being lectured by dear friends with their little bottles of water and their regular visits to the gym," she said in a 2007 interview with the *Washington Post*:

"All of a sudden, we've got this voluntary prohibition that has to do with health and fitness." She paused. "I'm not really in favor of health and fitness."

But isn't it good to be healthy?

"I suppose so," she replied, "but it's largely a crapshoot. The ghost of my sainted mother hovers around, talking about how self-centered it all is. They're always thinking about themselves—how far I ran, how much I can bench-press, how I ate three servings of broccoli. For heaven's sake, get over yourself."[26]

Holland died at age seventy-seven from lung cancer, having published more than fifteen books.

St. Leopold Bogdan Mandić (1866–1942) was a Croatian Capuchin friar and priest who stood a mere four feet five inches, suffered from chronic arthritis, and spoke with a severe stammer. He sat in the confessional for up to sixteen hours a day, listening to people bare their souls, counseling penitents, dispensing wisdom and love. "A priest must die from apostolic hard work," he once said. "There is no other death worthy of a priest."

That's not balance. That's love.

We're culturally conditioned, in other words, to expect the same worldly results from prayer—"balance," calm, self-satisfaction—that we try to get from eating well and exercising. There's nothing wrong with working toward physical health; in fact, we're called in a general way to be good stewards of our body. But Fr. Mandić didn't sit in the confessional for up to sixteen hours a day in the hope that he'd be relieved of his chronic arthritis, or of his stammer. He sat in the confessional because that was his vocation and because his deepest desire was to serve God whether or not he was in pain, whether or not he looked good in the eyes of the world.

Nothing more graphically illustrates this detachment from physical well-being than Christ offering himself up, in the prime of his life, to be brutally tortured to death. "Woe to you, scribes and Pharisees, hypocrites," he tells us. "For you clean the outside of the cup and of the plate, but inside they are full of greed and self-indulgence. You blind Pharisee! First clean the inside of the cup, so that the outside also may become clean" (Matthew 23:25–26). "Do not fear those who kill the body but cannot kill the soul; rather fear him who can destroy both soul and body in hell" (Matthew 10:28).

What the world means by "balance" is straddling two worlds: having our cake and eating it, too. Prayer consists in presenting ourselves, whole and entire, to receive the stupendous gift of God's love. Prayer consists in an utter surrender to God's will and an offering of our entire selves to his service. "You shall love the Lord your God with all your heart, and with all your soul, and with all your strength, and with all your mind; and your neighbor as yourself" (Luke 10:27).

Jacques Lusseyran, Blind Hero of the French Resistance

When you said to me: "Tell me the story of your life," I was not eager to begin. But when you added, "What I care most about is learning your reasons for loving life," then I became eager, for that was a real subject.[27]

—Jacques Lusseyran

And There Was Light is the strange and beautiful autobiography of Jacques Lusseyran, "blind hero of the French Resistance."

Born in Paris in 1924, Lusseyran lost his sight at the age of eight in a schoolroom incident. Even at that young age, he was groping toward the transcendent.

He came to learn that inanimate things are alive, and of the sympathetic current that runs between the branches of a tree in springtime, and that if you press the little stone you've secreted in your pocket, it will press back.

He wrote,

As a child I spent hours leaning against objects and letting them lean against me. Any blind person can tell you that this gesture, this exchange, gives him a satisfaction too deep for words.

Touching the tomatoes in the garden, and really touching them, touching the walls of the house, the material of the curtains or a clod of earth is surely seeing them as fully as eyes can see. But it is more than seeing them, it is tuning in on them and allowing the current they hold to connect with one's own, like electricity. To put it differently, this means an end of living in front of things and a beginning of living with them. Never mind if the words sound shocking, for this is love.[28]

In 1940, the Germans invaded France. Jacques, seventeen, continued studying for the entrance exams to *L'École Normale Supérieure* from the back bedroom of his parents' apartment. From that same bedroom he also mobilized fifty-two of his friends to form an underground youth resistance movement known as *Les Volontaires de la Liberté*.

He was betrayed by a member to the Gestapo. Jacques's dearest childhood friend, Jean, died under torture. Lusseyran himself was interrogated, imprisoned for six months, and sent to the concentration camp at Buchenwald.

Of his fifteen months there, he observed,

> That is what you had to do to live in the camp: be engaged, not live for yourself alone. The self-centered life has no place in the world of the deported. You must go beyond it, lay hold on something outside yourself. Never mind how: by prayer if you know how to pray; through another man's warmth which communicates with yours, or through yours which you pass on to him; or simply by no longer being greedy. . . . Be engaged, no matter how, but be engaged. It was certainly hard, and most men don't achieve it.[29]

A nonbeliever would scoff at the notion that a stone, a leaf, a tomato, presses back, but that awareness is precisely the quality of character that allowed Lusseyran to survive the camps. That childlike sense of mystery and wonder is the oil with which we keep our lamps lit. There is nothing soft about it. It is founded upon—and gives rise to further—profoundly disciplined action and thought.

Furthering our own self-interests requires a certain amount of discipline. But the kind of discipline exercised by the follower of Christ has a completely different focus and goal from the normal discipline we use to better ourselves.

The discipline of the follower of Christ consists of choosing hope over despair, forgiveness over retaliation, patience over anger, self-reflection over condemnation of others, the eternal over the temporal—no matter the worldly cost. To follow Christ is to insist upon seeking out the beautiful, the good, the true. It is to silently praise a tree rather than vociferously argue about bipartisan politics. It's to choose a half hour of quiet over three hours of mindless television. It's to take the last place rather than maneuver to wrangle the first.

To make all those seemingly small, seemingly insignificant choices toward life instead of death every minute of every day, over time, is to establish our house on solid rock. That is how the character of a man like Lusseyran is constructed, bit by tiny bit.

The Scandal of Miracles

For some extraordinary reason, there is a fixed notion that it is more liberal to disbelieve in miracles than to believe in them. Why, I cannot imagine, nor can anybody tell me. . . . [I]n truth this notion that it is "free" to deny miracles has nothing to do with the evidence for or against them. It is a lifeless verbal prejudice of which the original life and beginning was not in the freedom of thought, but simply in the dogma, of materialism.[30]
—G. K. Chesterton

So constrained are we culturally by our boxes of science, technology, and the material that many are literally unable to imagine anything outside them. That a deeper reality may and does exist beyond or within this one is beyond such people's ken. They call themselves realists and not only jeer at but are offended by such ideas.

To believe in miracles requires a wide-ranging curiosity and a large-
ness of imagination. That explains why one group that doesn't jeer at
miracles is children.

Here's a passage from *The Velveteen Rabbit*, for example, the classic
by Margery Williams, which could have been written about Christ
himself. The stuffed animals are talking amongst themselves in the
nursery:

> "Real isn't how you are made," said the Skin Horse. "It's a thing
> that happens to you. When a child loves you for a long, long
> time, not just to play with, but REALLY loves you, then you
> become Real."
>
> "Does it hurt?" asked the Rabbit.
>
> "Sometimes," said the Skin Horse, for he was always truthful.
> "When you are Real you don't mind being hurt."
>
> "Does it happen all at once, like being wound up," he asked, "or
> bit by bit?"
>
> "It doesn't happen all at once," said the Skin Horse. "You
> become. It takes a long time. That's why it doesn't happen often
> to people who break easily, or have sharp edges, or who have to be
> carefully kept. Generally, by the time you are Real, most of your
> hair has been loved off, and your eyes drop out and you get loose
> in the joints and very shabby. But these things don't matter at all,
> because once you are Real you can't be ugly, except to people who
> don't understand."[31]

Still, a miracle isn't a magic trick. God isn't Santa Claus. A vision, for
example, in and of itself means nothing. So the Virgin Mary spoke to
you. And?

A miracle is what happens *as a result of* the experience. A miracle
has practical application. A miracle allows us to do something useful
that serves others.

That's why Christ seems to put more emphasis on the forgiveness
of sins—talk about a miracle!—than on physical healings. That's why

for a drunk to get sober is at least on a par with the lame man who throws aside his crutches and walks, or the blind man who sees, or the deaf man who can suddenly hear. In fact, the miracle is even greater, because true recovery from alcoholism consists in a healing that is not just physical but also mental, emotional, spiritual, and moral.

Here's why we scoff at miracles: our egos can't stand to think that things happen on a level we can't see, capture, measure, control, or sell.

So how can we be open to miracles? How do we deal with our egos that want to back off from and avoid that which we can't capture? What can we do to wake up and feel the universe pressing back?

We choose to take full responsibility for our lives. We let our desire go to the stars, we get honest with ourselves about what we truly long for, and then we order our lives to the smallest particular around those desires.

We stop saying, "Oh, I'd like to walk the Camino, but there won't be enough money" or "I've always wanted to be a writer, but people will laugh at me if I fail," or "I truly feel I was put on this earth to make stained-glass windows, but the kids need to go to Ivy League schools." The mark of a follower of Christ is a bold setting forth, in spite of our fears, on a rocky, lifelong pilgrimage.

But as soon as we take the first step, we are somehow shored up and guided on to the next step. Nothing opens us more surely to feel the universe pressing back than to follow Christ rather than the world. When I quit my high-paying job as a lawyer to follow my vocation of writing, I felt the universe pressing back with a full, hearty, and utterly sure embrace. The way has been long, circuitous, and often lonely. I've often felt unsure as to how to handle certain people, situations, decisions. I've often sorrowed because I couldn't feel or see that my work was bearing fruit.

But I have never, for one second, stopped believing that the entire crazy universe—all the flowers, all the birds, all the stars—is pressing back with one gigantic yes.

I live in a second-floor apartment in a big old Craftsman bungalow in Pasadena. My balcony overlooks a number of giant, old-growth trees. One recent autumn afternoon, I was studying the graceful design of the branches of one of them (whose name I'm sorry to say I don't know): the small flame-red leaves fluttering intermittently to the ground, the glorious trunk resplendent against the setting sun. I thought, *If this were the only tree in the whole world, people would sell all they had and travel halfway around the world to see it. Look at it! This stupendous, mysterious living thing that grows up out of the ground!* "Counter, original, spare, strange," as the poet Gerard Manley Hopkins put it in "Pied Beauty." I stood there for many minutes, pulsating with wonder.

Don't get me wrong. That I could marvel at a tree didn't mean that I wasn't on another level also seething with various kinds of anxiety, resentment, distraction, and dread. Christ never promised that we'd be euphorically happy every second, or permanently free from fear. He promised that he'd be with us until the end of time (Matthew 28:20). He said, "I have told you this so that my joy may be in you and your joy may be complete" (John 15:11, NAB)—whether or not we can "feel" the joy.

But just for that moment—I did feel it. The universe was pressing back.

✝

Lord, help me get out of my own way long enough to see that the whole universe is a love letter—both to me alone, and to everybody who lives now, has ever lived, and ever will live. Help me choose to take full responsibility for my time here on earth.

6

Where Two or More Are Gathered in My Name

Many of us are drawn to a falsely romantic notion of monasticism, solitude, or desert dwelling. The fact is that in walking an authentic spiritual path, we will be more alone—without even trying—than we ever wanted to be. Whether we're urban contemplatives or cloistered religious, we can't fly solo. That's why Christ gave us the Church.

> *Where two or three are gathered in my name, I am*
> *there among them.*
> —Matthew 18:20

The Homily I'd Give If I Were a Priest

I once wrote an essay called "The Homily I'd Give If I Were a Priest." An excerpt:

Here's how you know your life in Christ is bearing fruit.

In spite of your own suffering, loneliness, and pain, you're welcoming. You're warm. You're kind (or you're at least shooting for those things, and not just toward the people who can do something for you, but everyone).

You're in immediate, intimate contact with a few active drunks, someone who's headed into or has just emerged from a psych ward, an incarcerated felon or two, a young girl who's pregnant out of wedlock, several women who have had abortions and are in silent, excruciating mourning, at least one stripper, several people in desperately unhappy marriages, about to be evicted from their apartments, or dying, a minimum-wage worker or two, at least three people who are certifiably insane, at least one U.S. Army chaplain and one peace activist (even better if they're both priests and the latter is in solitary confinement in a federal prison), several homeless people, and a whole *ton* of gay people, transgender folks, and sex and love addicts of all stripes.

That just happens to be my circle. That doesn't necessarily have to be yours, but our model, as always, is Christ. Who did Christ hang out with? Drunks, prostitutes, tax collectors *who were thirsting for something better.* If our message is not intelligible to a person of average intelligence with the usual human problems—addiction, greed, lust, money worries, troublesome relatives—*who is thirsting for something better,* what good is it? Who or what is our work and our prayer for?

In short, we have to develop some practice where we're not flying solo. We're called to participate. If we try to get away to some place where it's just us and Jesus, or us and God, we're headed for trouble.

Here Comes Everybody

Catholic means "Here comes everybody." [32]
—attributed in popular lore to James Joyce, *Finnegans Wake*

Participation is the essence of true spirituality: in particular, participation that is (1) not to our specifications, and (2) with people we did not handpick.

That means we're called to open our hearts to everybody, to welcome everybody, to be available to everybody—if and when they want us.

That is part of our vocation of love—and it is not for the faint of heart.

Oswald Chambers (1874–1917), a Scottish Baptist and Holiness Movement evangelist, wrote a great little book, wildly popular in its day, called *My Utmost for His Highest*. He's kind of a scold, in a bracing way. For example,

> Your god may be your little Christian habit—the habit of prayer or Bible reading at certain times of your day. Watch how your Father will upset your schedule if you begin to worship your habit instead of what the habit symbolizes. We say, "I can't do that right now; this is my time alone with God." No, this is your time alone with your habit. There is a quality still lacking in you. Identify your shortcoming and then look for opportunities to work into your life that missing quality.[33]

> The first thing God does is forcibly remove any insincerity, pride, and vanity from my life. And the Holy Spirit reveals to me that God loved me not because I was lovable, but because it was His nature to do so. Now He commands me to show the same love to others by saying, ". . . . love one another as I have loved you" (John 15:12). He is saying, "I will bring a number of people around you whom you cannot respect, but you must exhibit My love to them, just as I have exhibited it to you."[34]

Getting Straight with God, Ourselves, and Each Other: The Sacrament of Reconciliation

Do not seek for anything; do not perform anything; do not intend anything. Simply accept the fact that you are accepted! If that happens to us, we experience grace. After such an experience we may not be better than before, and we may not believe more than before. But everything is transformed. In that moment, grace conquers sin, and reconciliation bridges the gulf of estrangement.

And nothing is demanded of this experience, no religious or moral or intellectual presupposition, nothing but acceptance.[35]
—Paul Tillich

Theology, philosophy, and science are wonderful, as far as they go.

But theology can tempt us to substitute our abstract ideas of God for God.

Philosophy can tempt us to yammer about theories instead of actually follow Christ.

Science continually aspires to solutions that eliminate our need for one another: a pill, an injection, a surgery, a life spent before a computer screen engaged in "virtual reality."

The tragicomic fact is that we are saved by one another. And part of the way we are saved is by coming clean with our consciences.

We can't come fully into harmony with ourselves, God, and the people around us until we've made a concerted effort to clear away the wreckage of our past and to make reparation for it. We can't know what our mission on earth is until our souls are realigned with true north: love, Christ.

All kinds of people can help with this: spiritual directors, sponsors, friends, priests.

Interestingly for the follower of Christ, the person who begins to help us clear away the wreckage of the past doesn't have to be Catholic. For years, in fact, I've availed myself of fellow sober alcoholics with whom to do general moral inventories. On that level—one broken human being to another, one sinner, if you like, to another—this works beautifully. In fact, this kind of being heard by (and in turn, listening to) a fellow alcoholic in large part led me to Christ and the Church.

But the personal conscience, formed by nothing higher than its own lights, has limits. It's one thing to tell another human being, for example, that you've had an abortion, if for no other reason than to get it off your chest, to say, *This is who I am and what I've done*; to get in the habit of rigorous honesty; to cultivate the discipline of examining one's conscience. It's wonderful to find no judgment—in fact, maybe the other person's had an abortion too—to find, *There, I said it out loud, and I haven't been ejected from the human race.*

It's another thing entirely to know that abortion is an egregious tear to the human fabric and to want to be clean with God, to be absolved from it. That's not going to happen in telling another person who may or may not see abortion as *any* kind of wrong. So early in my sobriety I saw that there was a general moral order, and then there was a specific moral order in which I was willing to be guided and instructed and to which I was willing to be obedient.

I saw that you can't just make up the moral order as you go along. You can't just go on your intentions, on what at first glance "makes sense." Oh, let's just be *free*, we tell ourselves. Let's do what we want *as long as it doesn't hurt anyone.*

Well, what does *hurt* mean? If there's no objective moral order, then there's no objective measure of what it means to hurt someone. One person is going to think promiscuity is fine, and another person isn't. One person's going to encourage cheating on your taxes; another's going to call that stealing. One person's going to think guns are the antichrist, and another's going to want to arm every student and every teacher in the name of protecting their loved ones.

So we need an objective moral order. We need a set of teachings that say, in essence, Just in case you were wondering, this is what love, as Christ taught it, looks like. We'll want to consecrate those teachings, that order, in time and space: thus, the sacraments. We'll need people to administer the sacraments, and in the Catholic Church, those people—themselves sacramentalized—are priests: ambassadors of Christ whose individuality, *qua* priests, is subsumed—not extinguished, but subsumed—in Christ.

In the sacrament of Reconciliation, that protects the confessor from mistaking himself for an oracle with some extraordinary or supernatural power of his own, and it protects the penitent from a priest who might otherwise interpose an *ad hoc* moral code of his own devising.

I have many times sat across from, and told some of my darkest secrets to, convicted felons, functional illiterates, gay ex-meth heads, and all sorts of ordinary folks like myself, to truly great effect. I have become friends with many of these people; they have been deeply loyal and generous friends to me.

But I'm not going to *kneel* before any of those people. That I *want* to kneel; want to be absolved and set right; that the Church is built, in a sense, upon that very desire, makes me know that my house is built on solid rock.

✝

Heavenly Father, give me the grace to put up with the many unpromising people I come across in the world and in your Church. Give me the grace to see how very unpromising I am myself.

7

I Call You Friends

I do not call you servants any longer, because the servant does not know what the master is doing; but I have called you friends, because I have made known to you everything that I have heard from my Father.

—John 15:15

Christ invites us, astonishingly, to a friendship with him. What do we bring to it? Are we as interested in him—his family, his story, his worries, his sorrows and joys—as we hope he is in us?

From Away

Back in my native New Hampshire a couple of summers ago, I heard an out-of-towner referred to as "from away." I knew the phrase, and all it conjured, well: the distrust of the stranger. The proprietorship that makes us think that if we've lived and worked the land in a certain place, then it's "ours" alone. The suspicion of all that is different, all that is new, all that threatens and challenges the life we know.

Lying in bed that night, looking up at stars, I thought, Christ is "from away." Christ is from about as far away as it's possible to imagine.

At the same time, as my friend Horace says, "My God doesn't mind if I swear. In fact, my God likes when I swear!" God isn't our peer, in other words, but he's our Friend. He walks with us, even though he is from so far away.

To build a friendship, both sides have to sacrifice a little, put in some work, exhibit a willingness to be vulnerable. You might have a "friend," but after you help her move and spend a long day together hauling stuff around, you're *really* friends. When you spend all day cooking and invite over some people you've heretofore known casually, and one person brings a hunk of cheese and another a bouquet of flowers, and you break bread together, those people become your friends—or are well on the way to becoming your friends.

What would a friendship be if all we did was bring to the other our problems? To build a friendship, we're called to admire all that is good in the other, to go through rough patches with the other, to say thank you to the other.

So if we want to be friends with God, we develop a prayer life. We spend some time with him.

There are masses of books on prayer that describe the types and methods and stages and how to become an expert pray-er *who gets results* that will catapult you to number one in your convent, parish, office, new evangelization circle, book club, or media empire.

I can't be of any help there at all. Talk of "winners" and "warriors" with respect to prayer is, to me, oxymoronic. Christ told us to be willing to take the last place, and for me that's never so much a matter of willingness as acknowledging that I'm there by default pretty much all the time. I'm no prayer warrior, or any other kind of warrior. I'm just a run-of-the-mill, deeply flawed human being who is terrified of not being loved, afraid of dying alone, and surrounded by people *who never act the way I want them to.*

And who also really wants to be kind and to contribute—to serve, even.

Prayer is like writing. We either do it or we don't. Talking about it, reading books about it, talking to other people who do it isn't writing—and it isn't prayer.

Clearly, we're not going to be doing other things while we're praying. Clearly we turn off the TV, step away from the laptop, and put away the phone. I like to light a candle and a stick of incense, a little ritual to mark that I'm about to enter consecrated time and consecrated space. I live in a small one-bedroom apartment in which my consecrated space happens to be The Green Chair. You'll find your own.

Then the best way I know is just to sit down and talk to God, or open yourself to him, or do whatever feels comfortable or urgent or natural in the sense that you couldn't hold back even if you wanted to.

Love is like that.

I'm a morning person by nature, but whatever our circadian rhythm, prayer as soon as possible after we rise is definitely the way to go. I usually start my morning prayer with a thank you, have a little chat—this usually consists of, "Oh, Lord, I'm *so tired*"—and ask him to guide my thoughts, guarding me (even though if I've been awake for more than five seconds, it's kind of too late) from self-pity, dishonesty, selfishness, and pride.

One type of prayer consists in set words. Here, the Church is a treasure trove.

Prayer with Words

The Divine Office

You seduced me, LORD, and I let myself be seduced.
—Jeremiah 20:7 (NABRE)

The times I've spent in solitude have been some of the happiest of my life: a week at a hermitage cabin at New Camaldoli Monastery in Big Sur; a month at the top of Dorland Mountain in Temecula,

California; several days at the Desert House of Prayer outside Saguaro National Park.

It was at one such retreat, at St. Andrew's Abbey, outside L.A. on the edge of the Mojave in the late '90s, that I learned about the Divine Office, also known as the Liturgy of the Hours.

If you don't know about the Divine Office of the Catholic Church, you are missing one of life's great mysteries and joys: psalms, feasts, memorials, solemnities; saints and holy days; birth, death, resurrection; the whole cyclical pageant of the liturgical, and human, seasons.

Traditionally prayed at several set "hours" of the day—among them Vigils, Lauds, Vespers, and Compline—the Divine Office is recognized by the Catholic Church as a special form of prayer. The Second Vatican Council emphasized that the Divine Office should be the prayer of laypeople as well as priests, monks, and nuns.

To be thus invited made me feel, and still does, quite important, and from that moment forward I have prayed at least Morning Prayer pretty much every day.

Who would not want to have lines like these imprinted on their minds and hearts to help get them through another day of screaming kids, traffic, Pharisee bosses, and mindless FB feeds?

> My tears have become my bread
> by night, by day,
> as I hear it said all the day long:
> "Where is your God?"
>
> —Psalm 42

> At the end of the sky is the rising of the sun;
> to the furthest end of the sky is its course.
> There is nothing concealed from its burning heat.
>
> —Psalm 19

> The bows of the mighty are broken,
> while the tottering gird on strength.

The well-fed hire themselves out for bread,
while the hungry batten on spoil.
The barren wife bears seven sons,
while the mother of many languishes.

—1 Samuel 2:5

You can get a one-volume *Shorter Christian Prayer* that follows the basic four-week cycle, or you can troll eBay, as I did, and get the full-on four-volume set that includes Advent, the Lenten and Easter seasons, and two volumes of Ordinary Time.

Lectio Divina

Community means caring: caring for people. Dietrich Bonhoeffer says, "He who loves community destroys community; he who loves the brethren builds community." A community is not an abstract ideal.[36]

—Jean Vanier

Lectio divina is a fancy term for reading and reflecting on the Gospels. To me, the Gospels are living water, so this is no big chore. I don't make a project out of it or think of it as some special, exalted practice. The Gospels make Christ come alive. Why *wouldn't* we want ceaselessly to pore over, ponder, and reflect on them? Why would any human being deprive him- or herself of this inexhaustible font?

There are zillions of commentaries, guides, and so forth to help you with specific steps of Lectio divina. Take advantage of every last one of them, if the spirit moves, as it has often moved me.

But at the same time, don't let anyone tell you that he or she is needed to interpret the Gospels for you. Part of the genius of the Gospels is that they find us where we are. If your heart is open and sincere, God will reveal himself to you through them.

If you're famished for meaning and thirsting for truth like a dying man in the desert, there you will find it—in the Person of Christ. You won't need a PhD in theology. You won't need a self-promoting, new-evangelizing media celebrity whose message either scares the crap out of you or encourages you to think that if you pray really, really hard for your wishes to come true and mount a social media campaign, you can persuade God to make things go your way.

I emphasize the Gospels because they are the record of Christ's life on earth. He is always the model for our own behavior. His teachings always point the way toward either resolving, or accepting that we can't resolve, any conflict or problem that might come up in our daily lives.

To read the Gospels is to discover that the way, the truth, and the life are infinitely broader than the narrow, rule-based "religion" that many of us settle for. To follow Christ is to adopt an existential stance, a stance toward reality.

You may be surprised to discover that Christ, for example, said very little about sex. You'll find that he did say volumes about human nature, the human heart, and human relationships, and that those teachings are often deeply counterintuitive and always deeply useful.

You'll find that Christ spent most of his life healing, teaching, and hanging out with those who wanted to be called to a higher way of life. He got a kick out of all the things we do—eating, drinking, swapping stories, telling jokes—and he got the right kind of kick because he was utterly united to the Father in prayer. He made himself available to all kinds of very unpromising people—just as we're called to do. He had a special heart for those so desperate that they were willing to make holy fools of themselves in their hunger and need. Christ reveals himself in the deeply messy, profoundly awkward world of face-to-face human interaction with people in trouble, conflict, doubt, hunger, thirst, and pain.

The real encounter with Christ takes place not when we are all dressed up and polished and nicely groomed and brandishing our résumés but in our broken humanity. Encounter with Christ happens in our longing for a kingdom that is not of this world and that we must search for and work for with all our might in this world.

We're called to offer up our energy, time, and hearts—our very bodies—to "the poor": which is to say, people who, for all our intelligence backed by willpower, we are never going to be able to rescue, shape up, or "fix."

We'll find that Christ didn't moralize; rather, he observed that we're in bondage to the powers of darkness and death. We'll find that he spoke frequently and forcefully about money and the bondage of self, and we'll wonder why, in this culture of consumerism, materialism, and greed, we don't hear more in church about *those* teachings.

We'll find that he loved and closely observed nature, and we'll wonder why we're not more often urged to get away from our computer screens and out into the streets and the wilderness and the fields.

We'll find that over and over again Christ told us to be servants and to take the last place, and we'll see the falsity of all efforts to "evangelize" through marketing campaigns.

We'll find that the Son of man, the Hero-Sinless Victim, is the most compelling figure in literature, religion, and human history. We'll find that Christ is simultaneously way more liberal than the staunchest liberal and way more conservative than the most die-hard conservative. We'll find a personality that confounds, challenges, and instills wonder at every turn.

We'll come to agree with the Church's teachings, including those on the family, abortion, euthanasia, capital punishment, capitalism, usury, war, and violence of all kinds. We won't arbitrarily pluck out one or two isolated issues that happen to be easy for us to follow and ignore the many other teachings we'd rather not look at too closely because they might require the very kind of radical change we so vociferously demand of others.

"The crucifix requires no glove," as Emily Dickinson observed in an 1878 letter to a grieving friend.[37] Approach with hands that are open, bare, empty, and trembling.

But approach, approach, approach. Approach if you don't believe in Christ. Approach if you have no God, but approach. The more pain and doubt we're in, the better, simply because pain makes us hungry and doubt makes us humble. The scandal of the Cross lies precisely in the fact that Christ utterly exposes himself to the worst among us—and the worst in each of us. Christ says, Admit your faults, move forward doing the best you can, and don't worry about it—you've been forgiven.

We've been forgiven, and, even more unbelievably, we're loved so much that every hair on our heads is numbered. No one knew better than Christ that the pain against which we so desperately try to numb ourselves, and nearly all the world's evil, seem to stem from our terrible fear that we are basically unlovable.

The more we're grounded in the Gospels, the more inexorably we'll be led to the Church he established upon Peter, and we will be held safe and fast in her embrace and by her teachings.

We'll see that the Crucifixion and the Resurrection establish the final, cosmic triumph of love over fear.

If we're combing through the Gospels to pluck a single verse out of context in order to support, say, our right to own assault rifles, or our right to abort our kid, or our right to shun gay people, that's of course wrong. And the sad thing is that because we come with scheming hearts, all of the rest of the Gospels will be closed to us.

The Jesus Prayer

Having had my fill of listening, without acquiring any
understanding of how to pray unceasingly, I gave up on such
sermons that were geared to the general public. I then resolved,
with the help of God, to seek an experienced and knowledgeable
guide who would explain unceasing prayer to me, for I now found
myself so irresistibly drawn to learning about it.[38]
—Anonymous, *The Way of a Pilgrim*

One prayer that can become a kind of beat of the heart is the Jesus Prayer set out in the medieval classic *The Way of a Pilgrim* and immortalized by J. D. Salinger in the novel *Franny and Zooey*: "Lord, Jesus Christ, Son of the living God, have mercy on me, a sinner."

Some people have a heavy-duty aversion to seeing themselves as, or calling themselves, sinners. I don't know what to say to such people. I'm not *proud* of being a sinner—broken, flawed, in desperate need of help, mercy, and succor—but I have no trouble at all recognizing it. So to me, "Lord Jesus Christ, have mercy on me, a sinner," cuts right to the chase. First that Christ—suffering, love—is at the center of everything. Second, on my knees asking for mercy, I'm in right relation to him.

Which brings me to another interesting phenomenon about prayer: "When you are praying, do not heap up empty phrases as the Gentiles do; for they think that they will be heard because of their many words. Do not be like them, for your Father knows what you need before you ask him" (Matthew 6:7–8).

If God knows what we need before we ask, then why ask? It's true that he gives even if we don't ask. It's true that he bestows mercy on us anyway, all the time, whether we recognize him as the bestower or not. For my own part, I've come to see that my asking helps me *realize* that God is responding. My asking, again, puts me in right relationship to him and also helps cultivate a basic stance of gratitude.

I started praying the Jesus Prayer many years ago, and now I find that anytime I have a moment alone—in line at the grocery store, stuck in traffic, on the toilet is a very good place—I pick it up instinctively and realize that the prayer is repeating itself in my heart, always, carrying me along like an underground stream.

Like the anonymous pilgrim who brought it to our attention, I like best to say the Jesus Prayer while walking. It may be that as a woman I take smaller steps than a man, and thus have less time to say all of the prayer in rhythm to my heartbeat. But I usually leave out "Son of the living God"—and nothing bad has happened.

A Simple Surge of the Heart:
St. Thérèse of Lisieux

For me, prayer is a surge of the heart; it is a simple look turned
toward heaven, it is a cry of recognition and of love, embracing
both trial and joy.[39]
—St. Thérèse of Lisieux

St. Thérèse of Lisieux (1873–1897) was a bourgeois French girl, from a pious family, who entered a cloistered Carmelite convent at age fourteen, developed one of the truest inner lives the Church has ever known, and died an agonizing death from tuberculosis—unknown, unremarked upon—nine years later. She had no advanced education, no special charism. Her reading was largely confined to the Gospels.

She did, however, leave a record of her childhood and interior development, written under orders from her superior, that has since become the spiritual classic *Story of a Soul.*

Today, this "simple" young girl is one of only four women ever made Doctors of the Church.

Like recovering alcoholics, Thérèse knew she was too weak to go "up" to God; he was going to have to come down to her. She bore her many shortcomings with patience and grace. She often fell asleep during prayer in chapel, for example—Well, doesn't a child fall asleep in her father's arms? she thought—and let the matter pass. "If you are willing to bear serenely the trial of being displeasing to yourself," she wrote in a letter to one of her sisters, "then you will be . . . [for Jesus] a pleasant place of shelter."[40]

That childlike trust had metal at its core. She wrote the Apostles' Creed in her own blood and wore it next to her heart. She offered herself as a "Holocaust Victim"—to be consumed, used up, as God saw fit. She didn't concern herself with what level of prayer she'd achieved. She concerned herself with loving Christ. In fact, the deepest thing she ever said may have been, "There are no ecstasies, no raptures: only service."[41]

She also—major point in her favor—had a sense of humor. Her superior, Mother de Gonzague, once described her as a mystic-comic:

Tall and strong, with the air of a child, with a tone of voice and an expression that hide in her the wisdom, perfection, and perspicacity of a fifty-year-old . . . a little "untouchable saint," to whom you would give the Good God without confession, but whose cap is full of mischief to play on whomever she wants. A mystic, a comic, she is everything. She can make you weep with devotion and just as easily faint with laughing during recreation.[42]

Thérèse longed to be a martyr, a priest, a missionary, a saint. How to accomplish that in her obscure, dreary convent that was filled, just as our "cloisters" are, with the neurotic, the unkind, the difficult?

She realized that God's love for us is all invitation, untainted by the slightest shadow of violence. She realized that to resist making the other into an enemy and trying to dominate him or her is the highest possible spiritual practice.

We do, by the way, have enemies. Christ didn't say, "Everyone is our friend." He said, "Love thine enemies," the implication being, Don't worry, you'll have plenty of them. But we don't have to help things along by being hateful ourselves.

The way to help our enemies is to realize our own complicity in the evil of the world, to develop a deeply contrite and humble heart with respect to our own shortcomings and sins, and to throw ourselves utterly upon the mercy of God.

That's why Thérèse could say, "To pick up a pin for love is to convert a soul." She called her spirituality "The Little Way," but the point isn't so much that picking up a pin is a "little" act. Her point is that we don't have to have some huge charism or talent or gift. We don't have to be abnormally virtuous or to possess a superhuman capacity or desire for suffering. Her point is that when everything we do, think, or say in the course of our outwardly unremarkable day has Christ at the center, our whole life becomes a prayer that in the kingdom of God bears unimaginable fruit.

"My vocation is Love!" she realized. Why confine ourselves to one particular activity or way of being with God, in other words, to one form of service, to one group of people?

If I want to see how far I have to go in making love my own vocation, I have only to watch my reaction when, say, I've saved a seat for myself at a gathering and while I'm off chatting, someone else moves my stuff and grabs it. I have only to observe my inner state when another is praised in my presence, especially by someone who never praises me, and especially if the person being praised does the same kind of work I do. I have only to check out the spike in my blood pressure when the person in back of me makes a *super-irritating noise* while I'm trying to concentrate.

In fact, one of my favorite Thérèse anecdotes concerns her description of the woman who sat behind her in choir—the sisters' places were assigned for life—and made a supremely annoying noise, like "two shells rubbing together," possibly by clicking her rosary against her teeth, or because of ill-fitting dentures. Thérèse trained herself by the strictest discipline—the effort literally made her break into a sweat—not to turn around at the woman and glare.

Beyond Words: Adoration

Mrs. McIntyre's face assumed a set puritanical expression and she reddened. Christ in the conversation embarrassed her the way sex had her mother.[43]

—Flannery O'Connor

That "simple surge of the heart" eventually goes to a place beyond words. Not because we're embarrassed by Christ, like Mrs. McIntyre, but because the anguished cry of our deepest souls has no words.

Because prayer goes beyond words, it will look different for each of us.

From the outside, what it looks like each morning for me is something like this: After thanking God and asking him to guide my thoughts, I usually start with the Angelus, then Morning Prayer from the Divine Office, then I'll read that day's liturgy and reflection from *Magnificat*, a monthly magazine of daily readings and reflections.

That'll take maybe twenty minutes. Then I just sit. I don't do anything like count my breaths or try to empty my mind or say a mantra or anything like that. I just sit loosely but actively alert. I suppose in a way I invite God to think for me—except I'm not really thinking.

What happens during that time is beyond articulation. It's a mystery shrouded to me. It doesn't in any way depend on how I feel. Sometimes I feel consoled. Sometimes an insight will come. Sometimes I weep. Sometimes I'm impatient and distracted. My obedience and love are what matter, not my feelings.

I also know that one very good place for that kind of prayer is before the Blessed Sacrament. The consecrated Host—that is, the real Body of Christ—is always present in the tabernacle of a Catholic church (barring the last two days of the Easter Triduum). Many churches are open during the day so that you can sit quietly and pray.

Most churches also have set times of the week when the Body of Christ is "exposed" on the altar. The priest removes a single Host from the tabernacle and places it in a special vessel, usually gold with a round glass window, called a monstrance. The people worship—"adore"—Christ in his Real Presence in the Eucharist.

Recently I moved to the greater L.A. neighborhood of northeast Pasadena. Within a week, I'd discovered St. Elizabeth of Hungary, a church a half hour's walk from my apartment. Through a rose-bedecked courtyard I discovered the side chapel where daily Mass is said, and that is open daily from eight in the morning until nine at night.

I began to make my way on foot often to that holy space with its whitewashed walls and old-school Stations of the Cross, a red candle burning beside the tabernacle. In winter I walked through the dark, my coat buttoned against the cold. In spring, I walked at dusk. In summer, I walked during what photographers call "the magic hour," when the early evening light is a benediction.

That chapel has become part of my life. I often say Evening Prayer there, alone.

In silence, I realize how tired I am and think, *"Come to me, all you who are weary and are carrying heavy burdens, and I will give you rest"* (Matthew 11:28).

In silence, I realize how afraid I am, how hard of heart, how nonetheless saturated with longing.

How grateful.

Now I see that the whole reason an apartment materialized in that part of town may have been so that I would find my way to that chapel, so that I could sit with Christ in silence for a few minutes at the end of the day.

St. Thérèse of Lisieux was once asked by the Infirmarian at the Carmel what she said to Jesus when she prayed: "I say nothing," she replied. "I only love him."[44]

The Nightly Review

And so I repress myself, and swallow the call-note
of depth-dark sobbing . . .

Oh, and there's Night, there's Night, when wind full of
cosmic space
feeds on our faces: for whom would she not remain,
longed for, mild disenchantress, painfully there
for the lonely heart to achieve?[45]
—Rilke, *Duino Elegies*, "The First Elegy"

Each of us finds his or her own way and rhythm with prayer. But I do find that a short, nightly examination of conscience is very, very helpful.

Nothing complicated. First, last, and always: give thanks.

Then, I find that when I stop and get quiet, I know *exactly* where and how I was wrong during the day. I knew I was gossiping before the words even emerged from my mouth. I knew, as I was doing it, that I was trying to set someone straight. I knew I was trying to vanquish, triumph, get revenge, have the last word. I know when (always a zillion times) I was impatient. I know when I just had to make a little dig because I was jealous, even if the dig was only in my mind.

So I find it's a good thing to cop to all those things, give them to God, ask his forgiveness with a humble and contrite heart, put out my begging bowl one more time, and ask for help in doing better.

As I get older, I also find that I wake more and more during the night. Clearly, this is a call to prayer, and to deeper prayer. Under cover of night I can often be more honest with God. I can cry freely: sometimes with frustration and fear, sometimes with joy.

Christ and the angels visit us while we sleep.

✝

Dear Jesus, help me know that I'm allowed to approach you as I am, where I am, how I am. Help me remember that the crucifix requires no glove. Help me believe that you long to touch me, flesh-to-flesh, just as much as I long to touch you.

8

Go to Your Room and Pray in Secret

Whenever you pray, go into your room and shut the door and pray to your Father who is in secret; and your Father who sees in secret will reward you.

—Matthew 6:6

One huge temptation, especially for us attention junkies, is to make prayer into something we want to be noticed for. Nothing could be more obnoxious to those around us and surely to God. Christ himself went off to "a lonely place" to pray. Then he came back and helped people.

There Are No Rules—But for Heaven's Sake, Don't Make a Show of It

It seems there is a real desire, at the beginning of the spiritual life especially, to distinguish ourselves. For a long time, for example, I thought perhaps I was called to be a contemplative hermit. I really liked the sound of that phrase *contemplative hermit*. I'd always been a misfit; why not make it official? I'd always been most comfortable alone, recharging in solitude; why not make a decisive, dramatic break with the world?

How I identified with Thérèse who, of her time as an unpopular girl of ten at her abbey school, had written,

I didn't have, like the other former students, a *teacher friend* with whom I could go spend several hours. . . . Nobody paid attention to me, so I went up to the gallery of the chapel, and I remained before the Blessed Sacrament until the time when Papa would come to get me. This was my only comfort: Wasn't Jesus my *only Friend?*[46]

With that thought in mind, in the spring of 2007 I forsook the apartment in which at that point I'd lived for eighteen years, sold or gave away most of my belongings, and set off for six months on a cross-country pilgrimage. Perhaps, I thought, I'd find a community of some kind—people who would *want* and *understand* me. Perhaps I'd find a dear moss-covered hut where I could listen to the birds, pray the Divine Office, and commune with Jesus—my *only Friend!*—24/7.

Well, Jesus may be my only Friend, but I'm not his. If you in any way try to capture Jesus, to stay in the honeymoon suite together indefinitely, he will very gently at first, and then very firmly, pry your fingers off of him and shove you out the door.

After a forty-day silent retreat, the message I eventually got was, *Your place is in the world. That's where you're going to be of service. Plus, without human love, human attention, decent coffee, a good library, and the whole wack job minute-by-minute pageant of the human tragicomedy, you'd wither away in about five minutes.*

The goal isn't to distinguish ourselves; it's to disappear. My place is in the world partly because the world is where I'm to bear the most fruit, but also because interacting with others is where I work out my most drastic shortcomings, neuroses, and fears.

So I moved back to Los Angeles, resumed the life I'd built for myself over the preceding twenty years, and stumbled forward.

Since then, people occasionally have urged me to join this or that Third Order, or to take a formal vow of consecration, or to identify myself with some lay movement or religious community.

I find the better way for me is to live as far below the radar, and with as few labels, as possible. Nothing has formed me more perfectly than simply making myself available, insofar as possible, to whoever asks. Nothing has brought me closer to Christ than casting my lot with, and trying to serve, people I did not handpick.

As soon as you're a member of something or other, I find, the tendency is to exclude a whole bunch of people as not in keeping with the party line. Whereas my own path leads from L.A. skid-row drunks to Louisiana oil barons to Missourian seminarians and everyplace in between—and by path I don't just mean swooping in and giving an erudite PowerPoint presentation.

I mean sharing my experience, strength, and hope, one human being to another, with all the vulnerability, seemingly meager results, and constant sense of being overexposed, used up, and misunderstood that go with the territory.

Absolute Attention Is Prayer, and So Are Distractions

Attention, taken to its highest degree, is the same thing as prayer.[47]
—Simone Weil

Simone Weil (1909–1943) was a French mystic, writer, and intellectual who at one point insisted on working in a factory (though she was incompetent, loathed the work, and made no friends), was probably anorexic, and upon volunteering as a nurse in the Spanish Civil War promptly stuck her foot in a pot of boiling oil, causing burns from which she later, weakened by lack of food, fresh air, and human intimacy, died. Weil was famous for refusing to join the Church because she preferred to be in solidarity with the souls in hell: the patron saint of Those Who Do Things the Hard Way, a club of which I count myself a charter member.

I like her observation that absolute attention is prayer. That means that gardening, writing, cooking, and cleaning can be prayer.

But to say that absolute attention is prayer doesn't mean that if our attention is divided, we're not praying. If we're sincerely trying to pray, setting aside time to spend with God, allowing that simple surge of our hearts to go to God both in the time we specifically set aside for prayer and continually through the day, then we can be sure that God is working with, in, and through us, every second, to bring us more awake, more alive, and closer to him.

In *Prayer: Our Deepest Longing,* Fr. Ronald Rolheiser writes,

> A recent study on marriage points out that couples who make it a habit to give each other a ritual embrace or kiss before leaving the house in the morning and another ritual embrace or kiss before retiring at night fare better than those who let this gesture be determined by simple spontaneity or mood. The study makes the point that even if the ritual kiss is done in a distracted, hurried, perfunctory or duty-bound way, it still serves a very important function—namely, it speaks of fidelity and commitment beyond the ups and downs of our emotions, distractions and tiredness on a given day.[48]

So if you're bothered by inattention during prayer, welcome to the human race. If you're plagued by distractions, join the club. I pay zero attention to how "well" I'm doing in prayer. The phrase doesn't even compute. How "well" can you praise a flower or get a kick out of your kid?

At the same time, progress in prayer is probably marked by the fact that we're more and more drawn to prayer. We come to see that that time alone—the half hour in the morning, the solitary daily walk, the continual turning of our hearts and minds to God during the day, the pause at sunset to say Vespers, the nightly review—is as essential as bread.

We come to see that prayer is a good in and of itself. In fact, one of the biggest benefits of prayer is that while we're praying, we can't also be hovering, perching, spying, judging, managing, controlling, manipulating, and forming useless opinions that serve only to bring more discord to the world instead of more harmony.

Instead, the "absolute attention" to which Weil refers comes to mean being fully alert *all through the day* to the beauties of creation—while also ever more conscious of the reality beyond this one.

Certainly that will mean a respect for life, in every form, from conception to the grave. Certainly it will mean not having terribly more money and possessions than we need. Certainly it will mean putting allegiance to Christ infinitely above any allegiance to nation or state.

The More We Pray, the More We Can Afford to Be Misunderstood

One thinks of all the meaningless attitudes and gestures—in the name of God? No, in the name of habit, of tradition, custom, convenience, safety and even—let us be honest—in the name of middle-class respectability, which is perhaps the very least suitable vehicle for the coming of the Holy Spirit.[49]
—Fr. Alfred Delp

The more we're grounded in prayer, the more we can afford to let people misunderstand us. The more we also see there is always at least a kernel of truth to the way we are misunderstood.

Fr. Alfred Delp is the German Jesuit priest I mentioned earlier whose *Prison Meditations* are a classic. One incident, recorded in his diary for 1944, speaks volumes about his humility and his capacity for mercy. The Nazis were beating him and calling him "Liar!" because he wouldn't give up the names of his friends. He wrote, "I prayed hard, asking God why he permitted me to be so brutally handled, and then I saw that there was in my nature a tendency to pretend and deceive."[50]

Prayer gives us the kind of radical self-acceptance that allows us to admit, for example, I *am* kind of a liar. Or I'm not a very good mother, or husband, or nun, or writer, or follower of Christ, as the case may be. That doesn't mean we get to be slothful in prayer. We have to have tried, and to have longed with all our hearts, to be better, and to realize that we kind of can't.

For my own part, I am often unkind, often do angle to be the favorite, get attention, be first in line, hog the conversation.

So when someone accuses me of those things, or points them out, I also don't have to jump to the conclusion that the person is the antichrist.

This holding of the tension between the way we long to be and the way we actually are is the cross. We're nailed to our imperfections. We're attached, our whole time on earth, to our incarnate being that makes us naturally tend toward fear, greed, and lust.

That doesn't mean we ignore, in weary resignation, Christ's call to come higher. It means we try as hard as we can, knowing beforehand that we'll always fall short. It means developing a keen sense of humor about the gap between how we present ourselves to the world and how we really are.

In a March 10, 1956, letter to her friend Betty Hester, for example, Flannery O'Connor observed, "I hate to say most of these prayers written by saints-in-an-emotional-state. You feel you are wearing somebody else's finery and I can never describe my heart as 'burning' to the Lord (who knows better) without snickering."[51]

The late Monsignor Lorenzo Albacete wrote, "Have you noticed that many horrendous murderers and serial killers are said, at one time, to have been very religious? I always looked at my most pious altar boys with deep suspicion, wondering what was going on within their religiously agitated minds."[52]

And in his homily for December 15, 2014, Pope Francis said,

> I confess something to you, when I have seen a Christian, a Christian . . . with a weak heart, not firm, not fixed on the rock—Jesus—and with such rigidness on the outside, I ask the Lord: "But Lord, throw a banana peel in front of them, so that they will take a good fall, and feel shame that they are sinners, and so encounter You, [and realize] that You are the Saviour." Many times a sin will make us feel shame, and make us encounter the Lord, who pardons us, as the sick who were there and went to the Lord for healing.[53]

So we can give up trying to get spiritual straight As. Because, come on. This is *God*. Who do we think we're kidding?

As Fr. Damien says, "There's only one unforgivable sin. And that's to avoid God until you're in good enough shape to fool him."

What Does "Reward" in Prayer Mean, Anyway?

People often think of Christian morality as a kind of bargain in which God says, "If you keep a lot of rules I'll reward you, and if you don't I'll do the other thing." I do not think that is the best way of looking at it. I would much rather say that every time you make a choice you are turning the central part of you, the part of you that chooses, into something a little different from what it was before. And taking your life as a whole, with all your innumerable choices, all your life long you are slowly turning this central thing into either a heavenly creature or a hellish creature.[54]
—C. S. Lewis

Reward certainly doesn't seem to mean money, sex, or recognition, some form of which is often what we're looking for.

Nor does it mean some of the satisfactions that are perhaps subtler: the perfect spouse, kids who reflect well on us, a career as a famous spiritual writer or speaker. Our motives can be good—of course we want happy kids and a career that bears fruit—but those may or may not be the ways Christ chooses to bear fruit in us.

In fact, the kind of reward Christ is talking about seems to be a total forgetting of self. It's a movement away from the effort to surround ourselves with people and accomplishments that reflect well on us, to a spontaneous celebration of the way God shines in and through other people. The very realization that we're capable of celebrating—loving—someone besides ourselves *is* the "reward." We move away from the demand for peak experiences and begin to see that the kingdom of God—entering through the narrow gate—consists mostly in trudging, plodding, suiting up, and showing up so that we're available for the kind of "small moments" Fr. Damien describes below.

He's talking here about his early days in rehab:

Ralph saved my life. I tried to go to meetings with Ralph. It was months, going to every single meeting, three months into it that I had this experience. I associate it with one young man's share; I could see him at an angle, he was on the other side of the room. And he was just so happy. He was taking a chip to mark six months of sobriety. He was a young guy, and he'd told his story, and no doubt about it: he was a genuine alkie. And he was exuberant that he got to be sober. When he shared, he said, "I get to be sober. You *get* to be sober."

This is something I could not have *imagined* at this hokey, do-it-yourself amateur hour with other amateurs who are not as smart as you. But when you have to depend on people who are not as smart as you, you end up identifying with them so that your heart's touched, and you understand, you learn, about your own guts. And what's more important than learning about your own guts is becoming happy that another person's sober. And that stayed with me. Because what happened was, I rejoiced. With this young man on his six-month chip. I rejoiced with him. And I knew: *Something's different.* I'm no longer an observer in AA; I'm a member. I'm in, that's all. I'm in. That was the big deal. It was a movement from learning this, learning that, to being *in.*

A spiritual awakening is when you get happy that someone *else* comes to life. This is so profoundly healthy. You need to experience your own humanity. You need to calm down enough to be willing to live. Without a drink. Okay, you see. This can actually work. One day at a time, I can actually, probably live without a drink.

But you have to be renewed all the time, and you have to put yourself in a way of life where, for that hour in a meeting at least, you are willing to be bored to death 80 percent of the time. It's not 80 percent, really; it's less, but if it is 80, so be it. It's worth it because you have to have the moments of identification, to have your heart touched. You have a need to be connected to another person, in mutual respect and love, and to be happy that someone else is getting sober, and to know that you're being fed. I don't think the phenomenon is so much being loved by someone else. I never had that feeling of *Oh, they love me.* That was never the thing that helped me feel better. It was, I'll be darned, I'm not so isolated and such an into-myself weirdo that I'm just trapped here forever. I'm actually happy somebody else is sober. This is healthy. This is healthy enough so that you can stand and take up your spot on the face of the earth. It's that kind of thing. Sobriety.

That's one way of saying that our idea of "reward" changes. Our definition of a spiritual awakening unfolds and matures.

Sister Wendy Beckett, the nun who talked about art on PBS, has also for decades been a consecrated virgin and hermit living under the protection of the Carmelite nuns at Quidenham, Norfolk.

In October 1975, she wrote,

I can't find the right words, but what I want to say is: God is always coming to us, as totally as we can receive Him, but from every side. He comes in "life," just as it is. The as-it-isness is precisely how He comes. If we look for Him in certain patterns or forms, we only receive a fraction. Now for you, the natural tendency is to romanticize the way of His coming. Your self wants that, at least: at least that glory, the glory of holiness. And He says: No, I can't give myself, not fully, in *any* way that gives self a foothold. Nothing romantic or beautiful or in any way dramatic; nothing to get hold of, in one sense, because it must be He that does the getting hold. A terrible death in every way, destroying all we innocently set our spiritual hearts on: all but Him. So utter joy, in a sense that "romance" can never envisage. There are depths of self-desire—innocently—that He must empty so as to fill them; He is doing it, and you must set your thinking being to co-operate. . . .[55]

To that end, I like the prayer of the twelve-year-old girl, known only as "the child" in the Flannery O'Connor short story "A Temple of the Holy Ghost":

"Hep me not to be so mean, she began mechanically. Hep me not to give [my mother] so much sass. Hep me not to talk like I do."[56]

✝

Heavenly Father, help me remember to look for you in the as-it-isness of life. Help me see that there is nothing higher, and nothing harder, than simply being kind to the people with whom I come in contact every day: family, coworkers, neighbors, friends.

9

Let Him Who Is without Sin Cast the First Stone

The surest way to stop judging everyone around us is to take our own moral inventory. Looking at our resentments, secrets, and fears will give us so much material to work with we won't have time to nose into other people's business.

The Other Person Isn't the Problem. I'm the Problem.

The reason for all disturbance, if we look to its roots, is that no one finds fault with himself.[57]
—Dorotheus of Gaza, 6th c. Turkish monk

Spouses of active alcoholics are spiritual giants: they live with people who suffer from a devastating physical, emotional, and spiritual illness, and they love them. They've learned to live full, rich lives whether the alcoholic stops drinking or not.

They've learned that they didn't cause the disease, they can't control it, and they can't cure it. They've learned not to create a crisis in the drinker's life, nor to try to fend off a crisis if it's in the natural course of events.

They've learned that to scold, whine, criticize, judge, nag, guilt-trip, reproach, and complain are forms of violence that, like all forms of violence, simply don't work—either to get the alcoholic sober or to effect any kind of life-affirming change *in themselves*. They've learned to let the alcoholic take responsibility for his or her own actions, and to take responsibility for theirs. They've learned to keep the focus on what they do have the power to change: their own actions, attitudes, and lives.

It's taken me decades to begin to learn this critical truth. It's taken decades to see that the other person—alcoholic or no—is not my problem. I'm my problem.

Even so, I continually forget. Even so, I'm always looking for an exception. Oh, so the Nazis weren't the problem? The problem was the *death-camp victim*?

The Nazis were *a* problem. A monstrous, concentrated evil; a ruthlessly efficient death machine perhaps unsurpassed in the modern world. But as Viktor Frankl observed in *Man's Search for Meaning*, even in a death camp the human being has the freedom to choose his or her attitude.

Most of us aren't in death camps. Even so, my battle is never with another person. It's with reality.

If I'm trying to get another person to change, or deferring my happiness until another person has changed, in fact, I've already lost that battle, not because the other person is stronger or smarter but because the battle is with reality. The person hasn't defeated me; reality has.

My battle isn't whether I can manage, control, fix, or heal the other person—that's already settled: I can't. The battle is to be in right relation to God, to live in the reality of my desire to give all my soul, all my strength, to God.

If we have addictive tendencies on top of it, we can become obsessively, compulsively attached to fighting the (fake, already lost) battle of trying to change another person. Instead, we get to learn to direct our will *toward* God, not away from a particular person. The victory isn't to stop loving the person in question; it's to love God above all else. It's to detach *and* love. It's not to take a vow to act a certain way around the person or set the person straight by using the perfect words, or to expect them to read our minds and then get mad when they don't. It's to surrender to God.

"I am the vine, you are the branches. Whoever remains in me and I in him will bear much fruit, because without me you can do nothing" (John 15:5).

Nothing!

These spiritual principles hardly apply to alcoholism alone. The compulsive fighting of already-lost battles is the very hallmark of our times. Societal drug problem? Let's make drugs illegal and fight an armed war against them. Let's have a war against cancer, a war against poverty, a war against terror. Too many "bad guys" with guns? Let's arm *everybody*! An armed society is not a polite society. An armed society is a paranoid, deeply dangerous society. True courtesy is based on heart, not fear. True courtesy is voluntary, not enforced.

True courtesy stems from a pitched, incessant, concerted effort to respond to a world that is never quite the way we want it to be with a policy of creative nonviolence, which is one way of describing the love of the Trinitarian God in action.

The Crucifixion is the single greatest, most cataclysmically transformative act of creative nonviolence the world has ever known. The Crucifixion marked the cosmic victory of the explosive, infinite power of redemptive suffering over the fake, ephemeral "power" of so-called redemptive violence.

The victory applies to an alcoholic spouse or to global terrorism. Trying to improve or regulate anyone but ourselves, trying to go *mano a mano* with violence, never effects a lasting peace. It always, always leads to more violence.

Resentments, Secrets, Fears

The eye is the lamp of the body. So, if your eye is healthy, your whole body will be full of light; but if your eye is unhealthy, your whole body will be full of darkness. If then the light in you is darkness, how great is the darkness!
—Matthew 6:22–23

The way to help a sick person is to get better ourselves. The best thing I can do for a fellow alcoholic is to do the hard and continuous work of staying sober. That way, if and when the person shows up, I'll have something to give. The best way to be a peace-keeper, as in stopping war on a global level, is to keep peace in my daily life.

One way to keep peace is by looking at our resentments, secrets, and fears. Perhaps we even write them down. Perhaps we share them with another.

In fact, a priest friend of mine says that to consider our resentments, secrets, and fears—concentrating on our part in creating or maintaining the resentment, secret, or fear, not the other person's—is a wonderful way to prepare for Confession.

To set aside the other person's wrong and look only at our own doesn't mean that the other person, or the system, or the world, is 100 percent right, good, and true. So culturally geared are we toward worldly results—winning, being number one, coming out on top—that many people see the idea of looking only on our part, and leaving aside the other's wrongdoing, as an abdication of responsibility: a failure to "stand one's ground," a moral failing.

But to turn the other cheek, or when a man asks for your cloak to give your tunic as well, is not to be a doormat. It's to freely choose generosity. It's to say I can afford to let you think I'm a loser because I so firmly know I'm acting from love.

On the other hand, when we act from love, we love ourselves, too. "Give till it hurts" is a good idea as far as it goes, but if it veers into self-depletion or self-punishment rather than self-giving, something's wrong.

To be grounded in Christ is also to know that if we are sincerely doing our best, we are doing enough, are giving enough—that we are enough, period.

Acting Our Way into Right Thinking

As Tolstoy once said, it is easier to write ten volumes of philosophy than to fulfil one of the commandments.[58]
—Donald Nicholl

There is no other or deeper way of prayer than simply trying to live the Gospels.

But what does that look like in everyday terms? How to start?

How do we translate the bland, generic remarks we hear about being kind to our neighbor and living in joy into the daily events of our messy, hurried lives? What does loving our neighbor look like in actual practical terms?

Instead of blaming, judging, and criticizing everyone around us, we get to start by asking, What triggers me in the course of my day? What makes me anxious? What makes me angry? What makes me feel hopeless, sad, depressed?

This ongoing examination of conscience is the basis of Ignatian spirituality, twelve-step spirituality, and the Gospels.

And it yields some very interesting results. As my friend Rip says, "I used to sit around going, 'Can you believe how these jerks are screwing up the world?' Of course, I was snorting cocaine, watching porn, and stuffing myself with junk food at the time."

Similarly, for a few very unfortunate (for her) years, I had a room-mate. One morning I saw that the dish drainer was overflowing and immediately thought, *What a hypocrite! She's always talking about being neat, and she leaves all her crap for me to put away!* So I started putting the stuff away and after a few seconds realized that 80 percent of it was mine.

Still, self-examination is fine as far as it goes, but it doesn't go nearly far enough. I can know all kinds of distasteful things about my patterns of human interaction and be completely powerless on my own to change them. As it's been said, we can't heal our diseased thinking with our own diseased brain.

Still, the insistence on seeking beauty, the cultivation of a heart that feels the universe pressing back, the self-examination that gradually leads us to see the interconnectedness of all people, times, and things: these contemplative practices are not separate from the life of action. Rather, they lead our prayer, our thoughts, and our actions to become increasingly integrated.

So instead of thinking our way into right acting, we get to act our way into right thinking. Here are some ways that might work out in daily life.

Restraint of Tongue and Pen

Little children were being brought to him in order that he might lay his hands on them and pray. The disciples spoke sternly to those who brought them; but Jesus said, "Let the little children come to me, and do not stop them; for it is to such as these that the kingdom of heaven belongs." And he laid his hands on them and went on his way.

—Matthew 19:13–15

I love any biblical passage that has to do with children. If I hadn't been a broken-down drunk and lost child myself for so long, I don't know how I ever would have come to Christ. Child*like*—open, full of trust—though, not child*ish*.

Left to my own devices, I tend to take everything personally and react to all perceived meanness, abandonment, or rejection like a five-year-old. We don't have to pretend to ourselves that the wrong, or insult, or disappointment doesn't hurt: those things do hurt. I, for one, can seldom detach from the hurt in the fight-or-flight moment. But I do think that prayer, over time, enables me to get a little better at allowing myself to feel the hurt, absorb it, and move on.

I'll give one such example. One afternoon I was waiting to lead a little gathering of twenty or so spiritually minded women at which I'd been asked to speak. I was feeling my usual mixture of shyness and excitement. I took my seat and looked over to see a woman I'd spent many hours trying to help over the years and had gone out of my way to be kind to in spite of the fact that she has borderline personality disorder and belongs in a mental institution.

She took one look at me, heaved a melodramatic sigh, and loudly remarked, "Well, I hope you say something *new*." Oh, that was a harsh blow! When I was so looking forward, with a truly childlike heart, to sharing! When I'd tried so hard to go out of my way and be kind to her! My impulse was to snarl, "Listen, you vile, hateful shrew . . ." Instead I sort of chuckled and said, "Well, maybe I *won't* say anything new!" And smiled at her, and when the time came, I shared my thoughts with an open heart and moved on.

Miracle!

A related idea: we learn that we don't *have* to voice our opinion. We probably have one, but unless directly asked, we don't have to voice it. We can avoid all manner of drama—family disputes, work battles, internecine fighting in the church—simply by refraining from voicing our opinion.

We Don't Have to Set People Straight

My secret is very simple: I pray.[59]
—St. Teresa of Calcutta

Setting people straight is another form of psychological violence to which I, for one, am especially prone.

A radio interviewer, for example, will suggest as our time slot a Saturday 10:00 a.m. show and apologetically add, "I know how we love to sleep in Saturday mornings, but that's the only opening."

My impulse will be to set her straight. My impulse will be to take a simple statement as an accusation against which I have to defend myself. My impulse will be to reply, "Actually *I* rise at the crack of dawn. I pray. I make my bed. I'm at my desk by eight," when all I really have to say is, "Saturday morning will be fine. Thank you so much for thinking of me."

Or say someone asks us to a movie by a director we loathe. We don't have to say, "Are you kidding? I wouldn't waste my precious time watching that piece of dreck!" We can just say, "Thanks so much, no." We don't have to let the person know that he or she has bad taste.

Sometimes we know people who love to be the first with a piece of news. "Did you know Walter found an apartment?" they'll crow. Actually, we might know. I find that it's a little act of love to reply, "What wonderful news! Good for him!"

No Is a Complete Answer

Above all, my beloved, do not swear, either by heaven or by earth
or by any other oath, but let your "Yes" be yes and your "No" be no,
so that you may not fall under condemnation.
—James 5:12

To put it another way, "Say what you mean, mean what you say, don't say it meanly, and say it only once."

When our friend invites us to her potluck graduation party, for example, we don't have to reply, "I feel awful about saying no, but what with my incredibly successful career, I've been so busy lately" or "You know how I do all that volunteer work with prisoners" or "I've just been diagnosed with anemia and I'm *very* weak." We can just say, "Oh congrats, that is wonderful, and I'm so sorry, can't make it this time" (we don't have to add "or ever").

We learn to say a simple no with love. Otherwise, we invite a conversation, an engagement, that we really don't want. When we elaborate on the no, the other person is likely to ask, for example, "Can't you take iron pills?" or "You visit the prison on *Sundays*?"

A related tool, for when someone puts forward an opinion that makes our skin crawl, is a cheerful, "You could be right!" (We don't have to tack on at the beginning, "You're not right. But in another solar system populated by unfeeling cretins [you could be right].")

Or a thoughtful, "Huh, I never looked at it that way before." (We don't have to add "Because only a person with an IQ of 37 and a complete lack of human decency, common sense, and humor *would* look at it that way.")

Another great way to avoid engaging in a fruitless "conversation" is to respond, "Interesting!" Period.

Putting these tools into action introduces us, as a friend of mine puts it, to a "win-win God." What's good for me is also good for the other person—even if the other person doesn't like it.

If our choice is between guilt if we say no and resentment if we say yes—go with the guilt. Because guilt is not a good reason for saying yes. And we never have to feel guilty if we're humbly acknowledging, and bravely taking responsibility for, our humanity.

Wait for the Question

We hear that some are conducting themselves among you in a disorderly way, by not keeping busy but minding the business of others.
—2 Thessalonians 3:11 (NAB)

Here's another useful tool for those of us who pride ourselves on our ability to read minds: wait for the question.

For example, "He wants to ask me out, but he's too emotionally damaged, so just to help him out, I'll stalk him." "She wants me to quit my job, move cross-country, and adopt her child, but she doesn't have the skills to ask so she's using code and simply telling me the kid's having trouble in math class." "He wants to ask to borrow money, but he's too shy, so I'll send him some, then be pissed that he spends it on a trip to Vegas."

My friend Bill talks about the concept of "failed help": offering help where the help hasn't been asked for, then being resentful because the help isn't (1) accepted, (2) used in the way we think it should be used, or (3) responded to with deep, continuous, and undying gratitude.

So wait for the question. I find people are amazingly able to ask for just what they want: companionship, money, for you to quit your job, move cross-country, and adopt their kid.

They seldom do ask.

W.A.I.T.: Why Am I Talking?

[Jesus] would withdraw to deserted places to pray.
—Luke 5:16

If you're anything like me, you have spent untold hours "counseling," "listening," "advising," and "commiserating" with people who—though they've ostensibly sought your help—have not the slightest intention or desire of changing their behavior one iota.

So the question becomes, "Why am I talking? What am I trying to do here, really?"

Some of us are especially prone to a kind of emotional promiscuity, a tendency to over-attach, a thinly disguised craving to bestow a *special* kind of healing upon a certain person or people. This drive to attach and try to influence others can divide us from ourselves, God, and the other.

Whenever we refuse to be in the same relationship with the other that the other is with us, we commit a sin against chastity, in the global sense. We violate the other, and we violate ourselves. For example, perhaps we try to force our way into emotional intimacy by "sharing" too much about ourselves too early in the relationship. Perhaps we become possessive even though the other has made clear he or she is unavailable for and uninterested in emotional commitment. Perhaps we assume that just because we harbor deep feelings for the other, the other automatically harbors deep feelings for us. Perhaps we then feel it's our job to "help" the other express those feelings.

Pride makes everything—*especially* love—into a battle. I'm either going to rescue, fix, change, convince, or manipulate you into treating me the way I want to be treated, or I'm going to die trying.

Give the person with a problem who doesn't really want to change ten minutes, let the person know you love him or her, and hang up.

Don't Be a Doormat

Jesus said to him, "Why do you call me good? No one is good
but God alone."
—Luke 18:19

Christ was never a doormat.

We're not doormats either. We refrain from taking up an adversarial position in which one must win and the other must lose, but we're not doormats. We're not people pleasers.

Prayer gives us increasing courage to speak truth to power. And though power tends to bring to mind magistrates, policemen, and the NSA, maybe the power that keeps us most in bondage—and the situations in which we find it most difficult to refrain from taking up an adversarial position—is the power of our friends, work associates, and families.

Many of our families go generations, for example, without a single person acknowledging the elephant in the room of addiction, incest, or violence. Many of us spend our whole lives at careers we loathe, with spouses we wouldn't have freely chosen, with crushing debt for things and degrees that bring us zero joy because we were afraid of displeasing our parents or of being thought selfish, pushy, or unkind by our siblings or peers.

Standing our ground in the right way is a deep spiritual concept—a human obligation, in fact.

In *Holiness,* the late theologian Donald Nicholl wrote,

[O]ne of the features of responsibility that sometimes proves difficult to grasp is that it includes not only a subjective, personal aspect but also an objective, representative aspect.

I was first led to see this as a result of the years I spent in marriage counseling. During that time I gradually came to see that there was one factor in marital troubles that the textbooks on the subject hardly notice and certainly did not analyze sufficiently. That is to say, in almost all cases of marital breakdown I had an uneasy feeling that one or other of the partners seemed to put up with more from the other partner than he or she should have done. But it was difficult for me to find any ground for this feeling, since the "suffering" partner so very often appeared to be noble and to be putting up with the partner's bad behavior quite heroically. Then one day, after listening to a sorrowful tale from one of the "sufferers," I myself could not put up with it any longer and I exploded—silently exclaiming, "No human being should allow himself to be treated like that! As far as you personally are concerned you can put up with it if you like. That's your business! But you should never allow humanity to be insulted in that way. That's our business as well!" In the sufferer's person the image of man was being insulted and that somehow involved the whole of mankind. In other words, I saw that in all our actions there is both a personal and a representative element. Or, as the rabbis so neatly express it, "If I am here, then the whole of mankind is here." Which is not, as may seem at first, an arrogant statement but a sober formulation of a basic truth.[60]

Take a page from Jesus, who blew every system, including the family system, apart.

"Who is my mother? Who are my brothers?" he once asked. "[W]hoever does the will of my heavenly Father is my brother, and sister, and mother" (see Matthew 12:46–50).

His actual mother and his brothers were waiting outside at the time; he let them wait and continued with his healing.

Jesus treasured, reverenced, loved his mother. He crowned his mother Queen of Heaven and Earth. But his mother was not his god. His heavenly master was not his related-by-blood family.

The Holy Spirit Will Speak for Us

When they take you before synagogues and before rulers and
authorities, do not worry about how or what your defense will be
or about what you are to say. For the holy Spirit will teach you at
that moment what you should say.
—Luke 12:11–12 (NAB)

I'm a schemer. I also used to be a lawyer. So I've always been especially fascinated by the Gospel passage where Christ advises us, if we're hauled before our accusers, not to worry about what we're going to say.

For a long time I thought he was talking about an actual courtroom. I pictured Christ before Pilate, or the early Christians before Nero, or Maximilian Kolbe before the SS. But one day I realized that "the court" can also be the people in my everyday life with whom I so often find myself in conflict.

I don't have to build a case or mount a defense. I don't have to sit around figuring out what I'm going to say and hoping it will elicit such and such a response—at which point *I'll* say . . . we know how that goes.

Plus, I don't know about you, but whenever I make a "plan" to be snippy or to put someone in his or her place, it always gets blown to shreds. When I actually run into the person, one of two things happens: (1) my heart opens and I'm completely natural and kind, which makes me realize I've wasted all that time being mad and scheming, or (2) I've overthought the thing to the point that the resentment comes boiling to the surface and my face twists into a weird rictus of over-reactive hurt/rage that instantly reveals that I'm deranged.

So when "they" haul us before the court, we don't have to worry about what we're going to say. We can sincerely examine our conscience. We can run our conflict by a person or two whom we trust.

And we can let the rest go. When and if we're called to speak truth to any kind of power, the Holy Spirit will speak for us.

Hearing Someone Else's Inventory

As he went ashore, he saw a great crowd; and he had compassion for them, because they were like sheep without a shepherd; and he began to teach them many things.

—Mark 6:34

Fr. Damien calls hearing someone else's inventory "being in the presence of God in our real circumstances." He says,

> There was an inventory I heard from a woman thirty years ago, a large black woman, and she was going through her stuff, her resentments, fears, sex stuff. And she said, "Well I was doing my thing back then, I was turning tricks." And in the middle of it she stopped. She looked at me and said, "I was a poor whore." Meaning she didn't do a great job. And it struck me as so poignant. "I was a poor whore."

Aren't we all, I thought, harking back to the many, many times I have compromised myself in the most corrupt way, and by no means just sexually. On top of which, I didn't even compromise myself *well*. Just sort of hung around the edges: sad-sack; lackluster; one foot in, one foot out.

"That was one of the most spiritual things I ever heard," Fr. Damien continued. "We were both in the presence of God when she said, 'I was a *poor* whore.'"

For my own part, listening to someone else's moral inventory enlarges and enriches my spiritual life. The earnestness with which the other inevitably tells of his or her failings and wounds calls me to be earnest around my own conscience. The sincerity invites me to be more honest myself. The contrition welcomes *me* back to the table of the human family.

Cultivating a listening heart doesn't require belonging to any particular institution or program. A listening heart is a fruit of prayer. To be able to sit with the unresolved conflicts and challenges of another, to resist the impulse to fix and rescue, to be with the other in his or her suffering as a fellow sufferer is just what Christ did.

We may not be in a position to hear a "formal" moral inventory. But we are always in a position to be sensitive to the emotional and spiritual needs of the people around us. We can always be working to make ourselves more available, accessible, and present. We are always called to see ourselves in the other rather than to judge.

✝

Loving Father, grant me the willingness to face my own resentments, fears, and secrets. Grant me the courage to share them with another. Help me remember that love is not an ideal or an abstraction. Love consists in action.

Part Three

Resurrection: Getting Radically in on New Life

10

You Cannot Serve Both God and Mammon

Even when our motives are good, we can try to run the show. We learn that this tends to bring discord rather than harmony.

The Wrong Kind of Holiness

No one can serve two masters; for a slave will either hate the one and love the other, or be devoted to the one and despise the other. You cannot serve God and wealth.

—Matthew 6:24

Examining our motives is helpful. Observing that we often mask a bad motive under a good one—I'm purportedly trying to love you, but I'm really angling for you to love me; I'm purporting to "share information," but I'm really character assassinating—is incredibly helpful.

But the more we come awake, the more we realize that even when our motives are *good*, we often try to run the show.

Some people, for example, are over-attached to wealth. For a long time, I was over-attached to poverty.

I carried around a secret plan for my salvation. I imagined that one day, in a cataclysmically dramatic gesture, I would give away all my money (which, by the way, is, in the grand scheme of things, not much) to "the poor."

At last, I imagined, I'd be holy. At last, Christ would know I loved him.

Since then, I've come to see that my plan had me at the center, not Christ. Since then, I've come to realize that I would rather give my money to a set of unseen strangers with whom I don't have to interact than to share my money with people I know and love.

Poverty based on self constricts our hearts. Christ's poverty expands our hearts. When Lazarus's sister Mary anointed Christ's feet with expensive oil and dried them with her hair, Judas disapprovingly stood by and said, "Why was the oil not sold for three hundred days' wages and given to the poor?" He pretended to be for the poor, but he really wanted the money for himself. I pretended to be for the poor but really wanted spiritual riches (plus the security blanket of my money) for myself.

I wanted to be pure in a way it is not possible for anyone to be—and probably, given my wounds around money, especially not me.

Our money, and every other material and spiritual gift we've been given, is meant to bear fruit in the world—and not through gaining interest in some squirreled-away bank account.

What We Think Is Our Thing Often Isn't Our Thing

Why do you see the speck in your neighbor's eye, but do not notice the log in your own eye?
—Matthew 7:3

For a long time, I saw my tendency to hoard money (with the idea that I would someday, in one fell swoop, give all of it away) as a terrible spiritual block.

As I progressed in prayer, however, I began to see that I had many, many sins, character defects, and wounds that went way beyond my money issues. At some point, I had to look at the resentments, fears, secrets, and old ideas that threatened to keep me in the wrong kind of poverty in every area of my life, not just the financial one.

What we think is our thing, in other words, often isn't. Not what's deepest. Not what's really standing between us and God.

My thing was that I'd rather live in isolation and suffer doing everything by myself than participate. My thing is pride, in other words, and fear.

I'm so steeled for rejection and abandonment that I tend to skip over the whole messy middle part of interacting with the world, whereby I actually ask for what I need and thereby interact with other human beings. My thing, in other words, is trust.

My thing is that I tend to try to be holy in the way I think I should be holy, or want to be holy, or admire someone else for being holy. Except that my subconscious motive is that I want to look good. I want to perform some grand gesture. My thing, in other words, is grandiosity.

My thing is that I'm terrified there won't be enough, and thus I find it very hard to share. The fact that sharing doesn't come easily embarrasses me. My thing, in other words, is shame.

"I will do whatever you ask in my name, so that the Father may be glorified in the Son" (John 14:13). That's an astonishing promise, showing astonishing trust on Christ's part. But the more honest we are in prayer, the more sacred Christ's name becomes, and the less likely we are to ask for the wrong thing.

We ask to spend more time with him. We ask to become more like him.

Instead of clinging to the delusion that we'll make some grand future gesture—and *then* we'll be holy!—we begin to grab on to

Christ in whatever form he appears in daily life: old, young, poor, rich, crackhead, sex addict, soldier, peace activist, priest. We give God permission to use us as he will. And he takes us at our word when we do ask.

We'll take many pratfalls and learn many lessons through our desire to help.

Not long ago, for example, I met a guy who was trying to get sober. He looked fresh off the streets: scrawny, bad teeth, track marks.

My heart went out to him. I cornered him by the coffee machine, took his hand, and gave him my best stuff.

He was really getting it. I'd touched him, I could see it. I even leaked out a tear or two of compassion. Maybe he'd remember me five, ten, twenty years from now. *That woman who listened*, he'd think of me. *That woman who cared.*

Finally, I shut up. The guy looked at me, hard. "Wow," he said. "You have some really deep wounds, huh?"

That's a very representative illustration of my actual interaction with "the poor."

As Kierkegaard observed, "The more one suffers, the more, I believe, has one a sense of the comic."[61]

Mammon Isn't Money; It's Self-Reliance.

"How narrow is the gate, how strait the way that leads to death,
and few there are that find it" (Mt. 7:14). Did anyone know what
[Jesus] was really talking about? What was he to make of it, this
terrible failure to get people to respond? "I have come to set the
world on fire," he says, frustrated beyond measure because it doesn't
happen (Lk. 12:49). . . . And then Jesus begins to see that he
himself must drown in the depths of human misery, and that
through it God will work—how, he does not know. The grain of
wheat must die.[62]

—Ruth Burrows

Here's an example of how our motives can be sound and yet we can still be relying on ourselves—our will, our drive, our plan—rather than God.

A couple of years ago I was approached by a woman who proposed paying me to write a memoir of her life and work. We met, we came to an agreement, we worked for several months together. We had many phone conversations, which I taped and transcribed. I spent many weeks editing, shaping, fleshing out, piecing together a narrative.

I was glad of the work. I took the project very seriously, as I do all my work. I gave it everything I had. But in the back of my mind, after the third month or so, was a nagging, increasingly louder voice that kept whispering, "When am I going to get back to *my* work? *My* essays, my reflections, my next book? My voice, my interpretation of the world, *my* narrative?"

That went on for a couple of months. I was still working away, but the work had become just a bit of a grind. When am I going to get back to *my* work? That voice kept nagging.

I often start my morning prayer with the Angelus:

"Let it be done unto me according to Thy word." . . .

"And the Word was made flesh." . . .

"Pray for us, O holy Mother of God." . . .

One day, while I was contemplating the cosmic dimensions of Mary's yes, the thought came to me: *This* is *my work.*

I was being paid well. I admired the thrust of my client's vocation. My job, I realized, was to give her book everything I would have given a book of my own: all the heart, all the humor, everything that I knew and had experienced of the Christ of the Gospels.

I had heard the Angelus bell in my heart. Always, Mary is there to help steer us back on course. Always, in prayer, we learn one more time: "My yoke is easy, and my burden is light" (Matthew 11:30).

In fact, as time goes on, I find I'm less and less attached—as I was for a long time—even to "being a writer." Many opportunities for service have grown up around my vocation. So, more and more, I feel that whatever God puts in front of me is my work. Whatever writing assignment comes my way is "my" writing. Whoever passes through town and asks to have lunch with me is "my" work—and, of course, my sustenance, my mystery, my joy.

By the way, God uses whatever he can. My love for a free meal, as much as any purported self-giving, has motivated me to say yes to requests to meet for lunch or dinner many more times than I might have otherwise. And another connection is born. One more time, in spite of myself, I come to know him—and the person across from me—in the breaking of bread.

Another example of how "all things work for good for those who love God" (Romans 8:28): within the span of a couple of weeks recently, three women asked me to spiritually direct them. *How on God's green earth will I have the time and energy?* I thought, but something told me to say yes and trust that things would pan out. Our plan was to read and discuss a certain text, which meant, to my mind, setting up three different appointments each week.

Ordinarily, I would have prayed something along the lines of, "Help me do a good job." But this time, I saw that "Help me do a good job," at least the way I prayed it, carried a subtle implication of "Help me to look good. Help me not to screw up. *Make it so nobody can pin anything on me.*"

So instead I prayed, "Please give me something that will help these women. Be with us. Be in our midst."

Spontaneously, the three women somehow met and came up with the idea of all of us reading together. Which meant that instead of three appointments each week, I had one—plus all four of us gained from the shared reflections and fellowship.

More and more I wonder whether, at the end of the age, we're going to be asked not "Did you give all your money to the poor?" or "Did you set all the gay people straight?" or "Did you carry your pro-life placard?" but rather, "Did you sit down and share a meal with your friends? Did you have a laugh? Did you drink in this crazy, beautiful world to the last drop?"

Did you ever truly realize that your Father doeth the works—not you?

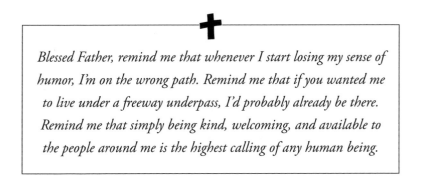

Blessed Father, remind me that whenever I start losing my sense of humor, I'm on the wrong path. Remind me that if you wanted me to live under a freeway underpass, I'd probably already be there. Remind me that simply being kind, welcoming, and available to the people around me is the highest calling of any human being.

11

Tempted in the Desert

Inevitably on the spiritual path we will come upon a situation that is so intransigent, so unresolvable, and so personally humiliating that we fear we've lost our way. One name for that state is the dark night of the soul.

Suffering Every Which Way

Waiting patiently in expectation is the foundation of the spiritual life.[63]
—Simone Weil

I've always had people with whom to walk the spiritual path. I have a faithful family and loyal, generous friends. But for years, I also suffered from an almost unendurable loneliness: what Fr. Ron Rolheiser—a favorite spiritual writer—describes as moral loneliness:

> Inside each of us, there is a dark memory of having once been touched and caressed by hands far gentler than our own. That caress has left a permanent imprint inside us. . . . And that dark memory, of first love, creates a place inside us where we hold all that is precious and sacred. . . . Paradoxically, it is the place where we most want someone to enter and yet where we are most guarded. . . . A fierce loneliness results—a moral aching. More deeply than we long for a sexual partner, we long for moral affinity,

for someone to visit us in that deep part where all that is most precious is cherished and guarded. Our deepest longing is for a partner to sleep with morally, a kindred spirit, a soul mate.[64]

Maybe that ache is what religion is. Maybe religion is what we do with our loneliness.

Whatever religion is, just as I turned fifty, and right after separating from my husband, I fell madly, crazily, annihilatingly in love with a guy who, let's say in a rather glaring understatement, did not feel the same way about me. At the time, I was also dealing with fear that my work wasn't bearing fruit, menopause, and every unhealed sexual wound I'd sustained in my long years in the bars.

I fell in love, and I also became obsessed. This tendency toward romantic obsession has generated untold amounts of suffering in my life. It's the part of me I'm most ashamed of, that touches upon my deepest vulnerability, that's most emblematic of an obviously egregious narcissistic wound, and that, over time, has seemed most impervious to healing.

The sixteenth-century mystic St. John of the Cross, in his classic writings on the stages toward mystical union, coined the phrase "dark night of the soul."

In one way, all of life is a dark night. Even the "easiest" human life contains more than enough suffering to develop a rich, deep inner life. But the dark night as described by John of the Cross, the way I understand it, comes when we've made a certain amount of progress, developed a fairly disciplined prayer life, and then come upon a situation that, no matter which way we turn, means excruciating suffering.

Should I disappear and never speak to the guy again? Hideous suffering. Should I stay and try to be "just friends"? Hideous suffering.

I had tried to read St. John of the Cross many times, with meager results. I'd highlighted, underlined, and made margin notes in *Ascent of Mount Carmel* until I was blue in the face, but somewhere between the night of the senses and the night of the spirit, the passive night and the active night, the three virtues, the three faculties, and the fifth way, the "desires harm the soul by making it lukewarm and weak, so that it has no strength to follow after virtue and to persevere therein," and I inevitably got sidetracked.

Again, Fr. Rolheiser came to the rescue, describing the mystical journey in language even a neophyte like me could understand. In *The Restless Heart* he observed,

> John of the Cross offers no painless way to enter loneliness and to come to grips with it. He is very realistic here. The inward journey involves pain, intolerable pain. According to him, once we stop trying to run away from our loneliness and stop trying to fill our thirsty caverns with counterfeit and pseudosolutions, we enter, for a time, into a terrible raging pain, the pain of purgatory, the pain that is felt when we cut ourselves off from pseudosupports and take the plunge inward, into the infinite mystery of ourselves, reality, and God.
>
> Eventually this journey leads to a deep peace, but in the early stages it causes intolerable pain. . . . Like all births, it is a journey from the secure into the unknown; like all births, it involves a certain death; and like all births, too, it is very painful because it is with much groaning of the flesh that new life can be brought forth.[65]

My "early stages" lasted about eight years.

In fact, my whole spiritual journey may be a pilgrimage through this particular wound of what used to be called attachment and what today we call codependence.

The Thin Line between Passion and Pathology

From time to time, [Blessed Franz Jägerstätter] would argue a point in the framework of an almost puritanical sexual morality. In his second commentary, written in St. Radegund before his

fateful decision, he draws an extended parallel between Austria's
unwillingness to take the risk of breaking her tie with an immoral
Nazi regime and a still halfway decent girl who has fallen under
the spell of an adventurer interested only in seduction, but who
finds it difficult to make the sacrifice a total break would involve.
Such a girl, he declares, can pray day and night and still not have
her prayers heard until she ends the relationship; and she may not
shrink back from any hardship even if he should threaten to kill
her or ruin her reputation.[66]
—Gordon C. Zahn

Around Year Five, I came to Fr. Damien. How could anyone have prayed the way I had, I basically asked, done the amount of inner work I had—the long years of soul-searching, the untold acts of charity, the fidelity to prayer—and still be so unbelievably flawed? Still over-impatient, still over-obsessive, still pining for what could not be, still triggered in the most embarrassing, unruly ways?

We were at Starbucks for coffee. He did his thing. He listened patiently. He closed his eyes. His head went to the side. Finally, he said, "We can't do hand-to-hand combat with our obsessions. We throw ourselves to the ground before them and peer around them to God. We pray for the obsession to be removed, and we consent to be disappointed when it isn't."

Then he thought for a minute and continued, "If you can accept that not one single thing about [this man you're interested in], or you, or the situation is going to change one iota . . . a space *might* open up where you can have some kind of mutually enriching friendship."

Acceptance is the answer to all our problems, in other words. The other person is not going to change. Why should he or she? That's not love; that's a monstrous attempt to make someone over to our specifications (which is wrong for exactly the same reasons that selective abortion, cloning, and eugenics are wrong).

But what's been even harder: I'm not going to change either—at least not to my specifications, and definitely not on my timetable. That we simply can't shape up ourselves the way we wish we could is one of the biggest crosses every human being carries.

I've undergone certain kinds and degrees of deep psycho-spiritual change. But the transformation, to date anyway, has never been, "Oh, now I've changed, and I'm only attracted to people who are 'sane' and 'healthy,' and when they can't reciprocate, I simply move on!"

I'm never quite sure what "sane" or "healthy" even means. Plus, I always feel that sane, healthy people haven't suffered enough and don't have a sense of humor.

From this situation and others, in fact, more and more my sense is that I'm called to lifelong celibacy.

But that's another story.

One thing I have learned: our prayer must always point to God, not to ourselves. Our love for our neighbors and for ourselves can be only as deep, rich, and wide as our relationship with the Father.

The solution can never be to try to "love" another less. The solution can lie only in loving God above all else.

Our Neuroses Don't Have to Be the Barometer

Now we see in a mirror, dimly, but then we will see face to face.
Now I know only in part; then I will know fully, even as I have
been fully known.
—1 Corinthians 13:12

Fr. Damien said another very helpful thing that day: "Whether or not the obsession is removed, we don't have to make the situation that we can't manage or control the absolute barometer of everything else."

For me, this came as a revelation. We don't have to make the situation we can't get rid of no matter how hard we try the biggest block, the deepest wound, the index of our spiritual health. When we're in the dark night, we don't have to think, *All the work I've done has gone for nothing.*

When we do try to make it the barometer, one problem is that we're constantly given to false hope: *I think he's finally warming up to me! I think my daughter is using less heroin! Progress!* Then the person reveals him- or herself to be exactly the same as he or she has ever been and ever shall be, and we're plunged anew into a cauldron of narcissistic torment.

So let's not make the unhealed aspects of ourselves the barometer of our spiritual health. The neuroses or the attachments may disappear; they may not. But to make them the barometer can only make them harder to bear, more frustrating, more intransigent, more impervious to healing. To beat ourselves up for being less emotionally or spiritually evolved than we might wish can only make for more anger, guilt, despair, sleeplessness, loneliness, and shame. More thinking that we can't love and aren't worthy of love, which is what spurs the insanity in the first place.

Maybe the hardest cross of all is our inability to sort out fully which of our actions stem from passion and which from pathology.

There are some aspects of ourselves, and our lives, we simply suffer. Staying connected to the material—food, faces, birds, trees—helps. So does continuing to give, even if all we often feel we have to give is our puny presence. We keep suiting up and showing up, no matter how lonely, frustrated, and misunderstood we might feel.

Like St. Paul's thorn, my tendency to find unavailable people to rescue and fix hasn't been fully removed either. So be it. If I could get rid of it, I would.

I'm sure God doesn't hold that against me.

Dame Margot Fonteyn: Prima Ballerina

Beauty will save the world.[67]

—Fyodor Dostoevsky

Dame Margot Fonteyn (1919–1991), prima ballerina, danced her whole career for the Royal Ballet. Like most of us, she also had a weakness. "She had very bad judgment about people," noted former assistant Colette Clark.

In 1937 Fonteyn fell madly in love with Panamanian playboy Roberto "Tito" Arias. They were married in 1955.

Fonteyn helped Tito smuggle guns (for which she was once arrested and briefly jailed) and overlooked his incessant philandering.

In 1964, Tito was shot and paralyzed, reputedly by the jealous husband of a lover. Fonteyn nursed him for the next twenty-five years, dancing into her sixties to pay his debts and support his family. The day he died, another of his mistresses committed suicide by drinking swimming-pool chlorine.

Soon after, Fonteyn was diagnosed with cancer. She converted to Catholicism on her deathbed so that she could be buried with him.[68]

Our culture pathologizes such fidelity, labeling it codependency or love addiction. But Fonteyn never violated her duty to her vocation. She gave her all to Tito while also giving all to the dance—and thus to us.

In the parable of the sheep and the goats (Matthew 25:31–46), Christ says we will be judged on whether we ministered to "the least of these." Did we visit the prisoner, give a drink of water to the thirsty, clothe the naked?

Matthew 25 reminds us that we will not be judged on our ability to evaluate character, nor on our powerlessness to heal our own attachments and addictions.

We will be judged on our capacity for mercy.

We will be judged on how much we tried to give in spite of our pain.

We will be judged on love.

Almighty Father, grant me the wisdom to remember that I'm not defined by my deepest wounds, my most painful compulsions, or my inability to figure out love. Help me participate and be cheerful even when I feel like I can't figure anything out.

12

Store Up Your Treasure in Heaven

One temptation in this culture of social media, self-promotion, and a numbers-based notion of success is to market our very selves as commodities. But let's not reduce our glorious humanity to a brand.

We're Human Beings, Not Brands

Do not store up for yourselves treasures on earth, where moth and rust consume and where thieves break in and steal; but store up for yourselves treasures in heaven, where neither moth nor rust consumes and where thieves do not break in and steal. For where your treasure is, there your heart will be also.
—Matthew 6:19–21

Those of us who make beauty through art have a special mission to hold the tension between the light and the dark. In order to make our way in the world, we're increasingly urged to have a platform, a brand, an advertising hook.

But we don't need to become commodities to make a humane living or spread the Gospel. We don't need to reduce our glorious humanity to an algorithm.

We're not brands because Christ isn't a brand. Christ is not reducible to a ten-point bullet program. Love has never claimed to be effective, clean, orderly, cost efficient, or formulaic.

Fr. Antonin-Gilbert Sertillanges, O.P. (1863–1948), the French Catholic philosopher and spiritual writer, wrote,

> How did the Savior proceed in his preaching? He offers no text, no system, and nothing organized or presented according to any order whatsoever. He presents himself, and it is he who is the doctrine and the truth. He permits himself to be seen, and that is already teaching; he acts, and that is teaching; he speaks, and the teaching becomes more precise, but without being fitted into the adapted framework of a system. His message exposes itself to the apparent chance of circumstances, and it is the ordinary environment of Jewish life that will be that of his apostolate.[69]

If Christ dared to move through the world without a system, a platform, a brand, *confident that his teachings would spread*, surely we can dare to as well. The cross is not marketable—and by the way, we all know how Christ felt about marketers in the temple. The cross blows apart every effort at commodifying, selling, promoting. Who would want to buy it? You can only want to embrace it for free.

Our whole culture, including Catholic culture, is based on a worldly model of marketing, numbers, approval, attention, and acclaim. So it really is the hero's quest to go our own way, in Christ, while simultaneously trying to lay down our lives for the people in a world that doesn't understand or usually even see us.

That doesn't mean we don't try to make a living. It does mean we sell our work: not an ideology, not a political affiliation or stance, not a movement, not a pose. The laborer *is* worthy of his hire. We deserve to be paid and paid well. Whether we are or not is a different matter, but to know we deserve it is to be in right relationship to God.

In the Apostolic Exhortation *Evangelii Gaudium* ("The Joy of the Gospel"), Pope Francis invites us to "recover the original freshness of the Gospel," finding "new avenues" and "new paths of creativity" without confining Jesus to our "dull categories."

When we shed the dull political, religious, and cultural categories, we begin to see God everywhere. Our eyes are on the hands of a different master than the cultural gods of money, property, power, and prestige. We transcend limiting political labels of right and left.

We begin to devote our lives to interesting, useful pursuits such as studying beetles, mason wasps, and praying mantises (Jean-Henri Fabré), building the Watts Towers (Simon Rodia), or writing a gorgeous, fully human book about an airport slum in India (Katherine Boo; *Behind the Beautiful Forevers*).

Wherever we are, and whatever our station, we pay attention to the people and things right in front of us. The late photographer Saul Leiter took most of his photos within a two-block radius of his Manhattan apartment, the streets of which he walked for decades.

Seymour Bernstein, a classical pianist from Brooklyn, gave up a promising concert career to teach. In the documentary *Seymour: An Introduction* (2014), he discusses his passion for music and his philosophy of life.

The guy's ninety. He lives like a monk. He's been practicing the piano for hours every day for decades. At one point, he's in conversation with author, religious scholar, and mystic Andrew Harvey. "I think the key," says Harvey, "is that music can produce ecstasy. And once you experience ecstasy, you can't be sold a shoddy bill of goods . . . You have the touchstone from which you can judge everything else."

Prayer gives us the increasing ability to discriminate between the true and the false, the authentic and the fake, the excellent and the mediocre, the vital and the inert.

Once we know that joy, we can't be sold a bill of goods.

Play from Your Heart

[You must] be renewed in the spirit of your minds, and to clothe
yourselves with the new self, created according to the likeness of
God in true righteousness and holiness.
—Ephesians 4:23–24

One of my heroes is the late comic Bill Hicks. My favorite clip is a jeremiad against market-driven conformity in which he scorns the squeaky-clean band New Kids on the Block and asks, "Since when did we do our kids a favor by teaching them *mediocrity*?" Then he falls to his knees and pleads, "Play from your *heart*. Play from your f-ing *heart*."

One form of mediocrity is the "happy ending." Happy endings sell. And the happy ending, by which I mean art in which the primary goal is to impart a "positive message," is a form of a lie.

The Crucifixion is not a happy ending; it's a surprise ending. The Resurrection is the biggest surprise of all. But the Resurrection is not a happy ending in the pleasure-based, self-based way that we define happiness in our culture.

Being in the world but not of it means that in one way we're always happy, and in another, we're always suffering.

As Fr. Damien says, "If you're lucky, you'll give up all hope of ever being happy in the way you thought you were going to be happy."

Thomas Merton, in a rare burst of dry humor, observed, "The man of solitude is happy, but he never has a good time."

And Andrei Tarkovsky (1932–1986), the Russian filmmaker whose works include *Andrei Rublev, Solaris*, and *Stalker*, wrote a wonderful book on art: *Sculpting in Time*.

In it, he observed, "The allotted function of art is not, as is often assumed, to put across ideas, to propagate thoughts, to serve as an example. The aim of art is to prepare a person for death, to plough and harrow his soul, rendering it capable of turning to good."[70]

That's the kind of "positive message" we can trust.

Ordinary Working People

No result of my work could please me better than that ordinary working people would hang such prints [of other working people] in their room or workshop.[71]

—Vincent van Gogh

If our message is not coherent and useful to a person of average intelligence with the usual human problems—addiction, greed, lust, money worries, troublesome relatives—what good is it? Who or what is our work for?

Prayer means nothing if its fruits can't be communicated to a person of reasonable intelligence and goodwill in a way that is completely relatable and understandable. What is our prayer for if we're not able to sit down with another human being, face-to-face, and say, "Tell me your story"? What is our purpose if not to make the lives of the people around us in this vale of tears a little easier to bear?

In Palm Springs one recent summer, desperate for company, I sought out a man named Jeff Mesinoff, who I happened to know lived in the area because he'd donated a few times to my blog.

It turned out that Jeff and his wife, Maxine, were the proud managers of the Royal Palms Mobile Home Park. With Christlike aristocracy of spirit, he and Maxine showed me around their domain, then took me into town and insisted upon treating me to lunch. Over crab cakes at Billy Reed's, they told me their conversion stories. They revealed themselves to be people of deep thought, deep insight, deep prayer, deep humor. They were keeping Christ's watch in Cathedral City, California. Over that meal shone a light, a beauty, an order. "They knew him in the breaking of bread," and we knew him that day.

After that lunch I thought, "Thank you, Lord. Now I have a picture of who I am writing for."

✝

Heavenly Father, grant me the grace to maintain my spiritual and vocational integrity. Help me remember that my job is to do your will, regardless of worldly success or acclaim. Keep sending people like Jeff and Maxine to show us the way.

13

Unless a Grain of Wheat Fall to the Ground

Nobody wants to die, literally or figuratively. But, over and over again, when we do consent to die to our own will, our own plan, our own people, we find that the world opens.

The Greatest Story Ever Told

I am on trial concerning the hope of the resurrection of the dead.
—St. Paul, Acts 23:6

I once heard a self-professed atheist admit, "The thing about atheists is we have no story." Compare that to The Greatest Story Ever Told. To believe is to have a story. Every conversion—and we are all converts—is an ongoing drama.

But the drama takes place on a level that is mostly invisible and unseen.

We work our tails off, for example, to raise a kid, to shepherd a parish, to write a book, and at the end we may or may not get even a simple thank you. To suffer; to wait, often a very long time; to be willing always to be led another way: that is Christ's way. The death to our egos is not a fake death. It's a real death, and it's ongoing.

"The gate is narrow and the road is hard that leads to life, and there are few who find it" (Matthew 7:14). That's not because God wants to make finding him hard but rather because we can't see the road beyond the gate—and we're afraid.

When we do find the gate, though, our whole being begins to align. We begin to come into harmony with reality. Prayer is no longer, if it ever was, an activity separate from life. Prayer becomes the beat of our heart, a state of being.

Just as the disciples didn't recognize Christ after the Resurrection, we often don't see the spiritual awakening, the Resurrection, either. We think we know what our awakening will look like, but we may not change at all in the ways we thought we'd change.

Still, perhaps we're a little more able to pause when agitated, more willing to ask for help, more apt to run the draft of our self-righteous e-mail past a trusted friend before hitting "Send."

We may become a little less likely to take offense; a little less likely to hold a grudge; a little more able to hold the pain of our jealousy, fear, or anger; a little less quick to set people straight. We need a little less to be thanked.

I've read a lot of books on mystical prayer. The authors speak of rooms in interior castles and islands and bridges and ladders, and they're often quite exclusive. As in, the surest sign that you haven't reached this room or island or rung of the ladder is that you *think* you've reached this room or island or rung of the ladder. Well, okay, and don't worry. But wouldn't the surest sign of authentic prayer be that the last thing we'd be spending our time on would be gauging whether someone else is as advanced as we are, or advanced at all?

Because, really, who cares? Tell me if I've missed the entire point of the Gospels, but the only reason for prayer is to get ourselves in shape to be available and kind to whoever shows up.

So my own deepest wish isn't to reach the third or fourth or fifth room of the interior castle. My deepest wish is to spare people from having to suffer from my character defects.

One afternoon a few years ago I was standing in line at my local 99 Cents Only store. I was tired, hot, and in a hurry, and the woman in front of me was taking *tons* of time: fumbling to unload her stuff, fumbling in her wallet, fumbling with the card reader, fumbling with her bags. I could feel myself, like a horse at the starting gate, poised to unleash an inner tirade of anger, frustration, and self-pity.

I remember making a conscious decision to say the St. Francis prayer instead:

Lord, make me an instrument of your peace. Where there is hatred, let me sow love; where there is injury, pardon; where there is doubt, faith; where there is despair, hope; where there is darkness, light; where there is sadness, joy. . . .

After what seemed like fifteen minutes but was probably three, the lady in front of me turned and said, "Thank you for being patient with me."

Me? *Patient?* That is probably the deepest mystical experience I've ever had.

Number one, I hadn't so much as exchanged a glance with this dear woman, but she had somehow felt from my body language, my breath, my being, that I *wasn't* pissed at her.

Two, that I wasn't pissed at her, that I had been patient for more than five consecutive seconds, had clearly come from a place so far, far beyond me that just for a moment, there in Aisle 5 with my coconut juice and fish-oil pills, the heavens opened.

Twenty years of prayer had borne a tiny, tiny fruit.

Help me not to be so mean. My prayer had been heard.

The Dawning—Let Us Pray—of a Just Peace

[W]hile [Catholicism] is local enough for poetry and larger than
any other philosophy, it is also a challenge and a fight. While it is
deliberately broadened to embrace every aspect of truth, it is still
stiffly embattled against every mode of error. It gets every kind of
man to fight for it, it gets every kind of weapon to fight with, it
widens its knowledge of the things that are fought for and against
with every art of curiosity or sympathy; but it never forgets that it
is fighting. It proclaims peace on earth and never forgets why there
was war in heaven.[72]

—G. K. Chesterton

On Ascension Sunday 2016, just after returning from Mass, I read
a piece in the *National Catholic Reporter* entitled "Landmark Vatican
Conference Rejects Just War Theory, Asks for Encyclical on
Nonviolence."[73]

The piece began, "The participants of a first-of-its-kind Vatican
conference have bluntly rejected the Catholic church's long-held
teachings on just war theory, saying they have too often been used to
justify violent conflicts and the global church must reconsider Jesus'
teachings on nonviolence."

I could hardly breathe. Finally, an expression of the simple, radical
teachings of Christ. Finally, a statement of the way, the truth, and the
life, from the personal to the global, that had led me to become a
member of the Church in the first place.

As Pope Francis has observed, "War is the 'mother of poverty.'"[74]

And as Dorothy Day, cofounder of the lay Catholic Worker movement, is reputed to have said: "Our problems stem from our acceptance of this filthy, rotten system."[75]

That filthy, rotten system, in which wealth is concentrated in the
hands of the few; power is used to oppress, punish, and humiliate;

profiteers and politicians feed off an ever-escalating cycle of violence, war, and death, is precisely the system Christ came to deliver us from.

If not—if he didn't change the entire vantage point from where, how, and why we live—then what *did* he come for? How did his coming have the utter existential, cosmic significance that I assume every follower of Christ believes it does?

To notice the filthy, rotten system is not to be a crank or an ingrate. It's to notice that the same system that oppresses the poor oppresses us. It's to be aware of our complicity in unholy systems and to realize that our choice of livelihood, for example, should perhaps weigh much more heavily on us than whether we voted Democrat or Republican. It's to remain ever aware of the terrible violence in our own actions, words, and hearts.

Those who espouse redemptive suffering over redemptive violence are often accused of living in some out-of-touch-with-reality dream world. In fact, the way, the truth, and the life are utterly practical. The teachings of Christ apply first, forever, and always at the personal level: to our daily interactions with our fellows; to our relationship to money, power, and sex; to our secrets, resentments, and fears that, unless we share them with God and another human being, fester, mutate, and resurface—as is true of all forms of terror and violence—into new, worse, forms of violence.

One of our deepest fears is that Christ isn't "enough": that the way, the truth, and the life are too small, too hidden, too inefficient to face down the evil in the world and in ourselves.

But if Christ taught us anything, it's that the world is always changed—and only changed—in the person-to-person encounter.

He saw how the world works. He knew how much, for example, we worry about money.

He said to regard the lilies of the field (Matthew 6:28–29). He said that your heavenly Father knows what you need before you ask (Matthew 6:8). He said not to store up your wealth in barns—fools!—because "this very night your life is being demanded of you" (Luke 12:20).

He emptied himself and took the form of a slave so that we no longer have to be slaves to this world. He said, Keep your eyes on the Master's hands, and he will show you how and where to go.

If we keep our eyes on the Master's hands, we allow ourselves to see that we don't have to be in bondage to our families. Christ said, Honor your father and mother, but you don't have to—out of obedience to me, you *can't*—sell your soul just to please your father and your mother. You don't have to put your life on hold, forever, in bondage to your father's and mother's old ideas.

We allow ourselves to go way below the surface and ask the deepest questions: about money, time, to whom and to what we order our lives. We see, for example, that we don't *have* to own homes. We don't *have* to send our kids to expensive schools where they learn, like some of us, to be the wrong kind of slaves.

He also said, "I have said these things to you so that my joy may be in you, and that your joy may be complete" (John 15:11). He knew how much we worry about loving and being loved. Of course we want to be approved, admired, loved; we *should* want to be loved. But we can't care so much that we allow our integrity to be compromised. We can't care in such a way that we mutilate ourselves in order to get the wrong kind of love.

To believe that Christ is who he said he was and that he meant us to live as he told us to live—that takes a soldier. "Take courage, I have conquered the world" (John 16:33). We don't have to commit violence against ourselves—against our hearts, our spirits, our questing, thirsting, ravenous souls.

Because when we commit violence against ourselves, we inevitably commit violence against others, whether in our personal or our public lives. Vatican PR aide Fr. Thomas Rosica, for example, has observed that sometimes online Catholic conversation is more "culture of death" than "culture of life."

> Often times the obsessed, scrupulous, self-appointed, nostalgia-hankering virtual guardians of faith or of liturgical practices are very disturbed, broken and angry individuals, who never found a platform or pulpit in real life and so resort to the Internet and become trolling pontiffs and holy executioners! In reality they are deeply troubled, sad and angry people. We must pray for them, for their healing and conversion![76]

Of course, we're called to see that often we are deeply troubled, sad, and angry ourselves.

While we're praying, we have to have a great capacity to be seen as losers, to be insulted, patronized, and persecuted—often as we are going without rest, pleasure, or inner peace to be faithful to our little policy of love, often toward the very people who are persecuting us.

No Satisfaction, Ever

Here we have no lasting city, but we are looking for a city that
is to come.
—Hebrews 13:14

Prayer doesn't make us more excellent. If we're lucky, prayer makes us more human.

For my own part, while others do the hard, saintly work of raising kids or going to prison for witnessing against nuclear weapons, I seem to be tailor made to sit at Starbucks, listening to some other lost, wounded soul's moral inventory or tale of woe. I'm the leper, they're the leper. It's so below the radar. Really? Yup. That's it. That's the kingdom.

All my fervent hopes to bring others into the Church and my deep desire to be recognized (the two are unfortunately connected) have come to absolutely naught.

Instead I've had friends tell me, "You're actually quite a decent person. What I don't get is how you can be *Catholic*." Another friend recently remarked, "He's the best kind of Catholic. *The kind who never mentions it.*"

I know what those people mean. But to be Catholic is to be between a rock and a hard place. The lover of Christ always wants to share her joy, her gratitude, her wonder.

The convert perhaps always goes a bit overboard.

So my friends suffer; I suffer. Let's just be there for one another in any small way we can. None of us feels understood. Every human being, even under the best of circumstances, lives in a kind of ghastly existential loneliness.

Let me ponder how I have contributed to that loneliness, to all suffering, with my own greed, my own sin. My ongoing hardness of heart. My three abortions. Let me try to be the mother my children deserved.

Fr. Damien says,

> I think we often perceive even the "service" we're good at as a failure. We're sitting with someone who's come to us for help, and what we perceive is that we're half-hearted and our attention span isn't very good. We're distracted by our own problems in the middle of hearing someone else's. We think that muddies up the whole thing. Well, that's the Cross. There's no such thing as the pure act. As humans, even our best intentions are always mixed with distractions, ambiguities. Forget the pure light. We get a flash of it.

One of my favorite stories about AA cofounder Bill Wilson—as told by Robert Fitzgerald, SJ—illustrates the point.

The year was 1940. Bill and his wife, Lois, were renting a small room above the 24th Street AA Club in New York. Things weren't going well. People who'd put together some sobriety were going out and getting drunk again. The organization was in dire financial straits. A nationally known baseball player had broken AA's tradition of anonymity by giving a story about his recovery, complete with full name and photograph, to a well-known newspaper.

At ten one night, Tom, the maintenance man at Bill Wilson's cold-water flat, announced the unexpected arrival of "some bum from St. Louis." Another drunk. Wearily Bill said, "Send him up."

Fr. Fitzgerald writes,

> As the man shuffled to a wooden chair opposite the bed and sat down, his black raincoat fell open, revealing a Roman collar.
> "I'm Father Ed Dowling from St. Louis," he said. "A Jesuit friend and I have been struck by the similarity of the AA twelve steps and the Spiritual Exercises of St. Ignatius."
> "Never heard of them."
> Father Ed laughed. This endeared him to Bill. Robert Thomsen tells the rest of the story this way in his book, *Bill W.*:

> > The curious little man went on and on, and as he did, Bill could feel his body relaxing, his spirits rising. Gradually he realized that this man sitting across from him was radiating a kind of grace. . . .
> > Primarily, Father Ed wanted to talk about the paradox of AA, the "regeneration," he called it, the strength arising out of defeat and weakness, the loss of one's old life as a condition for achieving a new one. And Bill agreed with everything. . . .
> > Soon Bill was talking about all the steps and taking his fifth step (telling the exact nature of his wrongs) with this priest who had limped in from a storm. He told Father Ed about his anger, his impatience, his mounting dissatisfactions. "Blessed are they," Father Ed said, "who hunger and thirst."

When Bill asked whether there was ever to be any satisfaction, the priest snapped, "Never. Never any." Bill would have to keep on reaching.[77]

Won't we all.

God Is Always Present in the Core of Things

As for [the seed that] fell among thorns, these are the ones who hear; but as they go on their way, they are choked by the cares and riches and pleasures of life, and their fruit does not mature.
—Luke 8:14

Christ knew it's often not the big traumas—sickness, natural disasters, financial shocks—that block us from the sunlight of the spirit. It's the daily cares and worries.

What if they're out of cherries?

That weasel still hasn't paid me.

My crown is coming loose.

We need to be in on something bigger than our self-centered obsessions and fears in order to avoid being overcome by them. We need community, the sacraments, liturgy, ceaseless prayer. We need all the help we can get.

Fr. Damien says,

As a recovering alcoholic, I haven't captured God but the big secret is that I'm in on something that is a gift to me. I identify with other people who are in on this gift, and there's a commonality with people who follow this path. It usually includes going in the direction of love and authenticity and honesty and away from arrogance and bragging. People who are sober in AA after horrendous failures have a way of keeping their subsequent successes right-sized. They might mention, "Oh I got my little pin at work for thirty years" but there's always a joke even about that. Always a sense of, "Can you believe? . . . *me?*"

Success is never accompanied by the arrogance of "I won the big prize." The sense is always of gift. I'm in on something deeper and wider than myself. God is in on this. And God is always anonymous, and God is always present in the core of things.

I associate my own being drawn in a special way into recovery, I almost have a picture of it. Forty-plus years ago, in rehab, I endorsed AA, but I didn't think I needed it because I thought I understood it! I was in my seventh institution, and I was going to meetings every day. I'm thinking, *I'm going to meetings, that's pretty good. They don't drive me nuts. I like 'em well enough* but [jabbing at his watch] *they better not go overtime.* The ambiguity of all that.

Then there was a period around the third month or fourth month where the realization came [he pauses, looks out the window, and a huge smile of dawning, I'll-be-darned delight comes over his face] . . . *You're in on it.* You don't possess it. You have to keep going to meetings. But you're in on it. There's a path here. It's a day at a time, and there are flashes of the divine coming out of other people's experience that light up your experience and help you to understand an aspect of your own thing. And this is *very healthy.* It's very sane. It's as close to anything authentic in human life that you'll ever find, so buddy, you better not go very far away from this.

I can't write it on a flag and wave it and say, "This is the way to go." I get in on something rather than possess something. The thing in me is that as soon as I get a good feeling, I want to capture it, tame it, possess it. But you don't possess the lover. You want to possess the statue, the jewel, the little . . . *What?* No!

God's universal. St. Francis was in on the authentic thing. But I don't know St. Francis personally. In an AA meeting, I'm hearing this guy right now. I'm with these people right here. The authentic thing is going on here. We want to capture that and wring it out and get the essence . . . well, forget that. We're in on it with our limitations and our blind spots, and we can't possess it, but we can say yes to it. We can say yes to the real thing. And know that we can't mean yes for every moment of the day and every angle of light throughout the day. But we can hook our wagon to it. We can say,

"Okay so what's the important thing about getting in on it that we can pass on to alcoholics who are at an AA meeting? 'Don't have a drink, right now, a day at a time. Keep coming back. Take the steps seriously.'" Actually do the work, even though this is action that by itself seems to be very unpromising. And we promise you that if you take this action, in a way we can't understand, you'll open yourself up to being touched, and to being a channel of encouragement to others. "Okay," I say. "Then I'd love to do that." Of course, right away I get a self-centered vision that's not the real thing. But the thing I can be in on is here all the same. So the two places in my life where I can say it's here are the Catholic liturgy and an AA meeting.

I always tell people that if, *in your mind*, there's a conflict between the God of AA and the God of the Church, go with the God of AA. *Because they're the same God.* If you take this thing as far as you can go, you will lay down your life for your friends.

The Persistent Will of Love

Every day crowds of unknown people come to him, who feel as hard, as cold, as empty as the tomb. They come with the first light, before going to the day's work, and with the grey mind of early morning, hardly able to concentrate at all on the mystery which they themselves are part of: impelled only by the persistent will of love, not by any sweetness of consolation, and it seems to them as if nothing happens at all. But Christ's response to that dogged, devoted will of a multitude of insignificant people is his coming to life in them, his Resurrection in their souls. In the eyes of the world they are without importance, but in fact, because of them and their unemotional Communions, when the world seems to be finished, given up to hatred and pride, secretly, in unimaginable humility, Love comes to life again. There is resurrection everywhere.[78]

—Caryll Houselander

Resurrection consists in a deepening participation with the world and with those around us: an ever-wider and deeper yes.

That ever-deeper yes leads us to ever-more-interesting discoveries.

That there is no time with God, for example, means that we can pray for the dead, and the prayer helps them as if they were still alive.

We consider God's economy and see that with God, nothing is wasted. Not an unpromising encounter, not a moment of suffering. With Satan, everything is wasted. Good is turned to wanton, senseless, mindless, barbaric, loutish, boorish, crude waste. Piles of corpses. Splattered blood. Families riven for no good reason. Loving brother set against loving brother.

At the same time, God is extravagant, and Satan is withholding and mingy. God never gives just the bare minimum. He gives more than we ask for. He pours out his love. So if we ask to help people, to open our hearts to the world, we don't have to worry. He'll shower us with opportunities.

We can look for opportunities to be in some small, invisible, loose way, of service. Not extra ways, just the ways that come to us and that come to anyone in the course of a day. I get lots of prayer requests, for example. I used to think, in my patient way, *What makes you think I have some special access to prayer?* or *What makes you think I have any more time to pray than the next person?*

Then I realized I'd been entrusted with a sacred honor. I started writing the requests down and keeping them next to my bed. That became a kind of practice for a few years. I'd take the requests with me into sleep, and when I woke in the middle of the night, which is often, I'd have the people who'd asked me to pray for them "in my heart and on my lips."

I don't do that anymore (though I do sleep with a rosary), but I've come to pay very close attention to prayer requests—because whenever anyone asks me to pray for him or her, it means *I* need prayer.

So you do a little extra thing, that costs. Teeny. You figure it out between you and God.

The function of those tiny acts and thoughts and prayers, over time, is that, very, very slowly we die to ourselves. Very, very slowly we become less focused on our will and more focused on God's.

It's taken me a long time to see that I'm an introvert who's been called out. I would always, always rather be alone and left alone—to read, ponder, putter, watch films, look at art, listen to music, pray.

Somehow God contrives to give me the silence and solitude I need, but I've also learned that the purpose of solitude is not my own personal spiritual consolation or advancement. The purpose is to equip me to serve others.

Through my writing and speaking, I've now come to hear from people from all over the world.

I hear from people who are passing through L.A. and want to have coffee; people who want to know how to get a literary agent, make a living writing, or overcome their fear of Catholic-culture judgment. I hear from people who want to get sober; people who want me to come visit their town, parish, or home; people who want to know what to say to their friend who can't stop drinking, who is having an abortion tomorrow, who is gay and can't tell anyone else, who is contemplating suicide, who wants to know the meaning of suffering, what the Real Presence means, and why I "chose" Catholicism.

I hear from people in Ireland, the Philippines, Australia, and Japan; in Montana, Kansas, Ohio, and Louisiana. I hear from people who are dying, whose spouses are suffering from Alzheimer's, who have cancer and are choosing to forgo treatment, who are longing for the right man or woman to come along; who've been fired, rejected, abandoned, shunned, scorned; who want to share their stories, their poems, their struggles, their sorrows, their hearts.

As best we can, in whatever way is given to us, we "sit" with whoever comes. We sit, but as Fr. Steve, friend to the elderly and infirm of suburban Boston says, "We don't sit too long." The disciples knew Christ in the breaking of bread—then he vanished from their midst (Luke 24:30–31).

He vanishes from our midst in prayer as well. For my own part, I seem not to be asking, seeking, or looking to sort things out quite as much as I used to. There is perhaps more of a trust, a proceeding in darkness in the absolute assurance that Christ is with me, that somehow everything will be all right.

Sometimes I think, *Shouldn't I come up with some big, important, new "way"—a synthesis of my life, thought, and work; a cataclysmic bringing together of people and ideas?* Then I remember: Christ already did that. Or rather he didn't do it—because there is no "synthesis." Christ *is* the synthesis.

And I circle back, one more time, to what I believe to be the greatest and the highest possible act of love: the shared meal. Breaking bread is simultaneously the simplest, most essential, most intimate ritual that we humans can perform for and with each other. To open my home and heart; to plan, shop, cook, serve, and clean up; to do a hundred little things each day to make my little apartment a nest of beauty and warmth *whether or not anyone shows up*; to welcome, celebrate, and connect the people I love to one another—all that has been one of the greatest fruits, if not the crown jewel, of my prayer.

Fr. Damien says,

Two things happen in prayer. The first is that there's a kind of unspoken joy in the way we welcome and greet people. Right away we trust that the other has it in them to respond to the invitation. We don't give people the bum's rush. We don't swarm people. We have a spiritual maturity.

The second thing that happens is the spontaneous urge to carry the message and to treat others the way we've been treated. If we've come to terms with our own brokenness, that "Yeah!" to other people's brokenness, escapades, sense of humor, remorse, and willingness to make things right is a profound spiritual experience. We have joy that someone else is coming alive; we're triggered into identification. People in whom prayer has taken root have a little bounce to their step.

People in whom prayer has taken root also love to dig into a good meal with friends.

Freedom without Asking Permission

In order to be free you simply have to be so, without asking permission of anybody. You have to have your own hypothesis about what you are called to do, and follow it, not giving in to circumstances or complying with them. But that sort of freedom demands powerful inner resources, a high degree of self-awareness, a consciousness of your responsibility to yourself and therefore to other people.[79]
—Andrei Tarkovsky, *Sculpting in Time*

That is what sobriety, and the Church, have given me: freedom. Freedom to be *in* this world—with all its terror and all its beauty—but not of it. Freedom to seek eternal life.

I'm sometimes asked by other women whether I'm bothered by the sexism of the Church. I'm always taken aback.

I don't think anyone would call me a shrinking violet. I've never been supported financially by a man. I've made my way in two areas—the law and publishing—that are dominated by men without sacrificing my integrity, my soul, or my sense of humor.

But demanding more of a voice, a higher place at the table, is simply not the way I approach the world. I'm forever at the back of the Church, saying, "I can't believe there's a place for me here" and "Lord Jesus Christ, have mercy on me, a sinner."

Nothing in this climate of rights, demands, control, choice, and entitlement could be more radically countercultural.

Nothing could require more fierceness, more intensity, more focus, more of a capacity to go one's own way.

Far from minimizing my womanhood, the Church has brought it to full flower. I write and speak from a Catholic viewpoint in a literary culture in which even to believe in God, never mind be a practicing Catholic, is career suicide. I have never written to or for any "market."

I've written of being a blackout drunk, of converting, of divorce, cancer, existential loneliness, and unrequited love, of cross-country pilgrimages, retreats-from-hell, and dinner parties that came as close to heaven as we get on our earthly pilgrimage.

In my weekly arts and culture column for *Angelus*, the magazine of the Archdiocese of Los Angeles, I celebrate filmmakers, composers, painters, conductors, ultramarathon runners, cyclists, skateboarders, trapeze artists, photographers, beekeepers, and portrait embroiderers.

My work doesn't fit into any one category. I have no platform, brand, sponsor, cheerleader, helpmeet, or benefactor. And the world has opened to me.

At a recent talk I met a young would-be writer who lives near me in a 1920s bohemian canyon with stone walls, cabins, and hiking trails. We arranged to have coffee.

I met a woman who lives on a sprawling family organic ranch near the Sespe Condor Sanctuary in Fillmore, California. "Come visit me," she said. "We'll have goat's milk, fresh eggs, citrus." So I did.

I received an e-mail from a woman who was born at Dachau and was to have died in a Nazi experiment to see how long babies survive after delivery when deprived of their mother and warmth. Would I like to hear more of her story?

To be open to all these encounters, to follow up, to be present to the people who ask, requires a tremendous outpouring of energy and love. I never especially *want* to follow up, but I'm always glad I did. I'm always the receiver. I'm always enriched and enlarged.

I'm also consumed. The power goes out of me. "My yoke is easy, my burden light"—*and* "Take up your cross." Love costs—it costs everything.

Through prayer, we undergo a psychic change but not a personality change. We're still triggered by the things we've always been triggered by. We still retain our basic temperament, affections, preferences, predispositions.

Christ still bore his own wounds after the Resurrection, and we still bear ours.

How else would other wounded people recognize us?

The Mystical Body

There are some people whom God takes and sets apart. There are others he leaves among the crowds, people he does not "withdraw from the world." These are the people who have an ordinary job, an ordinary household, or an ordinary celibacy. People with ordinary sicknesses, and ordinary times of grieving. People with an ordinary house, and ordinary clothes. . . . We, the ordinary people of the streets, believe with all our might that this street, this world, where God has placed us, is our place of holiness. We believe that we lack nothing here that we need. If we needed something else, God would already have given it to us.[80]
—Servant of God Madeleine Delbrêl

One way we know prayer "works" is that people come into our lives who show us the way and help call us higher. For me, some of those people are Tensie Hernandez and Dennis Apel, Msgr. Terry Richey, Ellen Slezak, Fr. Patrick Dooling, Julia Gibson, Rita Simmonds, Dr. Tim Flanigan, Fr. Tom Hall, Fr. Stephen Linehan.

Many priests. Many recovering alcoholics and addicts. People of integrity, kindness, loyalty, courage, creativity, perseverance, and heart, without whose friendship, example, and guidance I would wither and die.

The other way we know prayer works is that people come to us who are wounded. They may or may not come specifically for help. They may come for friendship and, as it transpires, not be quite capable of friendship. So be it.

My wounds around the search for love have been such a stumbling block in my life that they're always somewhat front and center. The good news is that working through those wounds, with the Eucharist at the center, has brought me more fully into solidarity with all of humanity than could possibly have happened otherwise.

Since coming into the Church twenty years ago, I've tried to remain faithful to her teachings, on sex and on everything else. I've stumbled; I've failed, but one thing this has given me is some rough purity of heart. I go to confession because I believe that what we do and think matters. I go because I believe someone, somewhere, needs me to be pure. Maybe it's the father of a ten-year-old girl who is contemplating molesting her. Maybe it's an adult who was abused by a priest as a kid and is about to abuse his own kid. Maybe it's the young men who are about to lynch Matthew Shepard.

A lot of people, I notice, come to me with sexual wounds: imprisoned sex offenders, pedophile priests, porn addicts. You could say, who *doesn't* have sexual wounds? But I think the attraction is no accident.

Recently, someone new came: Sawyer, a gay electrician who'd been shunned for calling out a couple of bullies in her queer community. She was newly sober, and she was in the dark night. Where was the meaning, the purpose?

As a twelve-year-old girl from a deeply dysfunctional family, she told me, she had read Judy Blume's *Are You There, God? It's Me, Margaret*.

Afterward, she was in such dread over the looming prospect of starting her period that she attempted suicide.

That one detail told of the pain and exile and fear and bewilderment in which she'd lived her whole life.

I was weary the day we talked. I was under a lot of stress. My whole body ached. But after my friend left, I knew to walk up to St. Elizabeth of Hungary and sit in the chapel for a few minutes before the Blessed Sacrament.

I could have driven the couple of miles, but voluntarily to undergo that teeny sacrifice, penance if you like—which also meant I could be refreshed by the flowers, trees, sky, and birds—was part of the continual miracle of the loaves and fishes that allows us, when we're giving, to receive, and when we're receiving, to give.

No one knew, saw, or cared that I had walked, that I had come, that I was in that solitary chapel with the afternoon light streaming through the stained-glass windows and the red candle burning by the tabernacle.

Like St. Thérèse, I didn't say much. I just loved him.

I walked home alone, as always.

I slept alone, as always.

But the next day I was able to call Sawyer and articulate something of what had come to me, alone in that chapel with my Savior, my Redeemer, my *only* Friend.

"That twelve-year-old girl you used to be?" I told her. "That's why we go on living. That's why we keep praying. That's why we stay sober and help another alcoholic. So some other desperate teenage girl or boy can live."

"So some other twelve-year-old girl we'll never meet doesn't have to kill herself."

✝

Loving Father, walk with me always. Whether or not I know the sweetness of consolation in prayer, keep me faithful. Keep me obedient. Keep me grateful.

Endnotes

1. Antonio Spadaro, SJ, "A Big Heart Open to God," *America*, September 30, 2013, www.americamagazine.org/pope-interview.

2. Flannery O'Connor, *Wise Blood*, Author's Note to the Second Edition (New York: Farrar, Straus and Giroux, 1990), n.p.

3. "Dana Gioia, California's New Poet Laureate: A Pew-Level Catholic," interview by Heather King, *Angelus*, March 18, 2016, www.angelusnews.com/articles/california-s-new-poet-laureate-a-pew-level-catholic.

4. Father Peter John Cameron, O.P., ed., *Magnificat Year of Mercy Companion* (Yonkers, New York: Magnificat, 2015), February 10.

5. Dom Mauro-Giuseppe Lepori, *Simon, Called Peter: In the Company of a Man in Search of God* (San Francisco: Ignatius Press, 2010), 128.

6. Flannery O'Connor, *Mystery and Manners* (New York: Farrar, Straus and Giroux, 1962), 34.

7. Jean Vanier, *Be Not Afraid* (Toronto: Griffin Press, 1975), 72.

8. Madeleine L'Engle, *Walking on Water: Reflections on Faith and Art* (Colorado Springs, CO: WaterBrook Press, 2001), 140–41.

9. William Harmless, SJ, *Desert Christians: An Introduction to the Literature of Early Monasticism* (Oxford, UK: Oxford University Press, 2004), 290.

10. Father Peter John Cameron, O.P., ed., *Magnificat Year of Mercy Companion* (Yonkers, New York: Magnificat, 2015), 277.

11. Alfred Delp, SJ, *The Prison Meditations of Father Delp* (New York: Herder and Herder, 1963), 190–91.

12. Meister Eckhart, *Meditations with Meister Eckhart*, ed. Matthew Fox (Rochester, Vermont: Bear & Company, 1983), 60.

13. Anne Frank, *The Diary of a Young Girl* (Ealing, UK: Bantam Press, reissue edition, 1993), 158.

14. Jean Sibelius, quoted by Alex Ross in "Apparition in the Woods: Rescuing Sibelius from Silence," *The New Yorker*, July 9, 2007, www.sibelius.fi/english/erikoisaiheet/dokumentit/ dokum_paivakirjat.htm. The diaries have only recently been released to the public and even so, in scattershot form.

15. William James, *The Varieties of Religious Experience* (New York: New American Library, 1958), 24–25.

16. Anne Harrington, *The Cure Within: A History of Mind-Body Medicine* (New York: W. W. Norton & Co., 2008), 109.

17. Jessica Diehl, "The Crowded Mind of Johnny Depp," *Vanity Fair* (January 2011), www.vanityfair.com/news/2011/01/ johnny-depp-201101.

18. Robert A. Johnson, *Owning Your Own Shadow* (New York: HarperCollins, 1991), 23–24.

19. Flannery O'Connor, in a letter to Cecil Dawkins dated December 9, 1958, *Flannery O'Connor: Collected Works* (New York: The Library of America, 1988), 1085.

20. Karl Rahner, *Theological Investigations XX*, 149. See also www.patheos.com/Resources/Additional-Resources/ Mysticism-and-the-Community.

21. Letter #638 from Vincent van Gogh to his brother Theo, July 1888, www.vangoghletters.org/vg/letters/let638/ letter.html#translation.

22. Alexander Liberman, *The Artist in His Studio* (New York: Random House, 1988), 6.

23. Philippe Petit, *Creativity: The Perfect Crime* (New York: Riverhead Books, 2014), 181–83.

24. G. K. Chesterton, *Orthodoxy* (Chicago: Moody Publishers, 2009), 196.

25. G. K. Chesterton, *Heretics* (London: Catholic Way Publishing, 2013), 84.

26. Peter Carlson, "She'll Drink to That," *Washington Post*, May 29, 2007, www.washingtonpost.com/wp-dyn/content/article/2007/ 05/28/AR2007052801400.html.

27. Jacques Lusseyran, *And There Was Light* (Sandpoint, ID: Morning Light Press, 2006), 3.

28. Jacques Lusseyran, *And There Was Light* (Sandpoint, ID: Morning Light Press, 2006), 27–28.

29. Jacques Lusseyran, *And There Was Light* (Novato, CA: New World Library, 1963), 269.

30. G. K. Chesterton, *Orthodoxy* (Chicago: Moody Publishers, 2009), 189–90.

31. Margery Williams, *The Velveteen Rabbit* (New York: Doubleday, 1922), 5, 8.

32. "Here Comes Everybody" was a sketch by Joyce from which *Finnegans Wake* eventually grew. "The first signs of what would

eventually become *Finnegans Wake* came in August 1923 when Joyce wrote the sketch 'Here Comes Everybody,' which dealt for the first time with the book's protagonist HCE." From the Wikipedia entry for *Finnegans Wake*, https://en.wikipedia.org/wiki/Finnegans_Wake. The entry quotes Luca Crispi and Sam Slote, *How Joyce Wrote Finnegans Wake: A Chapter-by-Chapter Genetic Guide* (Madison, WI: University of Wisconsin Press, 2007), 12–13.

33. Oswald Chambers, *My Utmost for His Highest* (Grand Rapids, MI: Discovery House, 1992), entry for May 12 (unpaginated).

34. Oswald Chambers, *My Utmost for His Highest* (Grand Rapids, MI: Discovery House, 1992), entry for May 11 (unpaginated).

35. Paul Tillich, "You Are Accepted," *The Essential Tillich*, F. Forrester Church, ed. (Chicago: University of Chicago Press, 1999), 201, emphasis added.

36. Jean Vanier, from the website for the L'Arche community: www.larche.ca/en/jean_vanier/daily_thoughts/theme/community.

37. Emily Dickinson, *Letters of Emily Dickinson*, ed. Mabel Loomis Todd (CreateSpace Independent Publishing Platform, 2015), 247.

38. Olga Savin, trans., *The Way of a Pilgrim* and *The Pilgrim Continues His Way* (Boulder, CO: Shambhala Publications, 2001), 2.

39. *Catechism of the Catholic Church* 2558, St. Thérèse of Lisieux, *Manuscrits autobiographiques*, C 25r. For a slightly different translation, see St. Thérèse of Lisieux, *The Story of a Soul*, trans. and ed. Robert J. Edmonson (Orleans, MA: Paraclete Press, 2006), 274.

40. *Collected Letters of St. Thérèse of Lisieux*, translated by F. J. Sheed (New York: Sheed & Ward, 1949), 303.

41. *St. Thérèse of Lisieux: Her Last Conversations* (Washington, DC: ICS Publications, 1977), 235.

42. Patricia O'Connor, *Thérèse of Lisieux: A Biography* (Huntington, IN: Our Sunday Visitor, 1983), 269.

43. Flannery O'Connor, "The Displaced Person," *The Complete Stories* (New York: Farrar, Straus and Giroux, 1971), 226.

44. St. Thérèse of Lisieux, ed. Paul A. Boer, Sr., *The Story of a Soul: The Autobiography of St. Thérèse of Lisieux with Additional Writings and Sayings of St. Thérèse* (CreateSpace Independent Publishing Platform, 2012), 2234–235.

45. Rainer Maria Rilke, *Rilke: Poems*, trans. J. B. Leishman and Stephen Spender (New York: Alfred A. Knopf [Everyman's Library Pocket Poets series], 1996), 165.

46. St. Thérèse of Lisieux, *The Story of a Soul*, ed. Robert J. Edmonson (Orleans, MA: Paraclete Press, 2006), 91.

47. Simone Weil, *Gravity and Grace* (London and New York: Routledge Publishing, 2002), 117.

48. Ronald Rolheiser, *Prayer: Our Deepest Longing* (Cincinnati, OH: Franciscan Media, 2013), 51–52.

49. Alfred Delp, SJ, *The Prison Meditations of Father Delp* (New York: Herder and Herder, 1963), 87.

50. Alfred Delp, SJ, *The Prison Meditations of Father Delp* (New York: Herder and Herder, 1963), 12.

51. Flannery O'Connor, *The Habit of Being: Letters of Flannery O'Connor*, ed. Sally Fitzgerald, (New York: Farrar, Straus and Giroux, 1979), 145.

52. Lorenzo Albacete, *God at the Ritz* (New York: Crossroad Publishing, 2002), 164.

53. http://en.radiovaticana.va/news/2014/12/15/
pope_francis_rigidity_is_a_sign_of_a_weak_heart/1114830.

54. C. S. Lewis, *Mere Christianity* (New York: HarperOne, 2015), 93.

55. Sister Wendy Beckett, *Spiritual Letters* (Maryknoll, NY: Orbis Books, 2013), 21.

56. Flannery O'Connor, *The Complete Stories* (New York: Farrar, Straus and Giroux Classics, 1971), 247.

57. Dorotheus of Gaza, *Doct. 13, De accusatione sui ipsius, 1–3,* http://dominicanidaho.org/meditation_dorotheus.html.

58. Donald Nicholl, *Holiness* (New York: Seabury Press, 1981), 88.

59. Mother Teresa, *No Greater Love* (Novato, CA: New World Library, 1997, 2001), 3.

60. Donald Nicholl, *Holiness* (New York: Seabury Press, 1981), 52.

61. Søren Kierkegaard, ed. Thomas C. Oden, *Parables of Kierkegaard* (Princeton, NJ: Princeton University Press, 1978), 30.

62. Ruth Burrows, OCD, *Essence of Prayer* (Mahwah, NJ: HiddenSpring, 2006), 138–39, emphasis added.

63. Simone Weil, *First and Last Notebooks: Supernatural Knowledge* (Eugene, OR: Wipf and Stock, 2015), 99.

64. Ronald Rolheiser, "Gethsemane—The Place of Moral Loneliness," February 20, 2005, http://ronrolheiser.com/ gethsemane-the-place-of-moral-loneliness/#.V4-zkflriM8.

65. Ronald Rolheiser, *The Restless Heart* (New York: Doubleday Religion, 2004), 121–22.

66. Gordon C. Zahn, *In Solitary Witness: The Life and Death of Franz Jägerstätter* (New York: Holt, Rinehart and Winston, 1964), 33.

67. Prince Myshkin, a character in the Fyodor Dostoevsky novel *The Idiot*, trans. Richard Pevear and Larisa Volokhonsky (New York: Vintage Classics, 2003), 382. Though the quote is often attributed to Dostoevsky himself, the passage from the novel comes from an exchange between Ippolit Terentyev and Prince Myshkin and runs as follows: "'Is it true, Prince, that you once said "beauty" would save the world? Gentlemen,' he cried loudly to them all, 'the prince insists that beauty will save the world. And I insist that he has such playful thoughts because he's in love now.'"

68. *Magnificat Year of Mercy Companion,* meditation for July 14.

69. A. G. Sertillanges, O.P., *Walking with Jesus in the Holy Land* (Manchester, NH: Sophia Institute Press, 1976), 64, 66, 67.

70. Andrei Tarkovsky, *Sculpting in Time* (Austin, TX: University of Texas Press Printing, 1996), 43.

71. Cliff Edwards, *Van Gogh and God: A Creative Spiritual Quest* (Chicago: Loyola Press, 2002), 61.

72. G. K. Chesterton, *The Everlasting Man* (Seaside, OR: Rough Draft Printing, 2013), 115.

73. Joshua J. McElwee, "Landmark Vatican Conference Rejects Just War Theory, Asks for Encyclical on Nonviolence" *National Catholic Reporter*, April 14, 2016, www.ncronline.org/news/vatican/landmark-vatican-conference-rejects-just-war-theory-asks-encyclical-nonviolence.

74. June 3, 2015, in his weekly general audience, www.catholicnewsagency.com/news/war-is-the-mother-of-poverty-pope-francis-says-80024/.

75. There is some disagreement as to whether and when Day uttered those exact words. See, e.g., Brian Terrell, "Dorothy Day's 'filthy, rotten system' likely wasn't hers at all," *National Catholic*

Reporter, April 16, 2012, www.ncronline.org/news/people/
dorothy-days-filthy-rotten-system-likely-wasnt-hers-all.

76. www.cruxnow.com/cns/2016/05/17/
vatican-pr-aide-warns-catholic-blogs-create-cesspool-of-hatred/.

77. www.barefootsworld.net/aafreddowling.html.

78. Caryll Houselander, *The Risen Christ* (New York: Sheed & Ward, 1958), 4–6.

79. Andrei Tarkovsky, *Sculpting in Time: Reflections on Cinema* (Austin, TX: University of Texas Press Printing, 1986), 180.

80. Madeleine Delbrêl, *We, the Ordinary People of the Streets,* trans. David Louis Schindler Jr. and Charles F. Mann (Grand Rapids, MI: William B. Eerdmans Publishing Co., 2000), 54.

About the Author

Heather King is a Catholic convert with several books, among them *Stripped*; *Parched*; *Redeemed*; *Shirt of Flame*; *Poor Baby*; and *Stumble*. She writes a weekly column on arts and culture for *The Tidings*, lives in Los Angeles, and blogs at www.Heather-King.com.

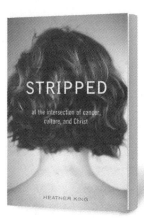

Additional Prayer Books

Sacred Space: A Little Book of Encouragement

4497-1 | PB | $12.95

Reimagining the Ignatian Examen

4244-1 | PB | $9.95

A Simple, Life-Changing Prayer

3535-1 | PB | $9.95

Hearts on Fire

2120-3 | PB | $12.95

To Order:

Call **800.621.1008,** visit **loyolapress.com/store,** or visit your local bookseller.

Continue the Conversation

If you enjoyed this book, then connect with Loyola Press to continue the conversation, engage with other readers, and find out about new and upcoming books from your favorite spiritual writers.

 Visit us at **www.loyolapress.com** to create an account and register for our newsletters. Or scan the code to the left with your smartphone.

Connect with us through:

 Facebook
facebook.com
/loyolapress

 Twitter
twitter.com
/loyolapress

 YouTube
youtube.com
/loyolapress